SAILING INTO THE UNKNOWN

SAILING INTO THE UNKNOWN

Sailing into the Unknown:

YEATS, POUND, AND ELIOT

M. L. Rosenthal

NEW YORK · OXFORD UNIVERSITY PRESS · 1978

Library of Congress Cataloging in Publication Data

Rosenthal, Macha Louis.
  Sailing into the unknown.

  Includes index.
    1. American poetry—20th century—History and criticism. 2. Pound, Ezra
Loomis, 1885–1972—Criticism and interpretation. 3. Eliot, Thomas Stearns,
1888–1965—Criticism and interpretation. 4. Yeats, William Butler,
1865–1939—Criticism and interpretation. I. Title.
PS323.5.R64   811'.5'09   77-10101
ISBN 0-19-502318-8

For permission to reproduce copyright passages grateful acknowledgment is
made to publishers and copyright holders as follows:

for T. S. Eliot: *Collected Poems 1909–1962* and *The Waste Land: A Facsimile and
Transcript of the Original Drafts Including the Annotations of Ezra Pound* edited
by Valerie Eliot, copyright © 1943, 1963, 1964 by T. S. Eliot; copyright © 1971
by Esme Valerie Eliot, reprinted by permission of Harcourt Brace Jovanovich,
Inc. and Faber and Faber Ltd.;

for Philip Larkin: *The Whitsun Weddings,* reprinted by permission of Faber and
Faber Ltd.;

for Ezra Pound: *The Cantos of Ezra Pound,* copyright 1934, 1937, 1948 by Ezra
Pound, and Ezra Pound, *Personae,* copyright 1926 by Ezra Pound, reprinted by
permission of New Directions Publishing Corporation ("In Exitum Cuiusdam"
and "Villanelle: the Psychological Hour" also appear in *Collected Shorter Poems*
by Ezra Pound; reprinted by permission of Faber and Faber Ltd.);

for W. B. Yeats: *Collected Poems:* "All Souls' Night," "The Tower," "Medita-
tions in Time of Civil War," "The Road at My Door," "Ancestral Houses,"
"The Stare's Nest by My Window," "I See Phantoms of Hatred and of the
Heart's Fullness and of the Coming Emptiness" ("I See Phantoms of Hatred
and of the Heart's Fullness and of the Coming Emptiness" also appears in *The
Variorum Edition of W. B. Yeats's Poems,* published by the Macmillan Co. of
London and Basingstoke), "Nineteen Hundred and Nineteen," "Sailing to
Byzantium," "First Love," and "Among School Children," copyright 1928 by
Macmillan Publishing Co., Inc., renewed 1956 by Georgie Yeats; "An Image
from a Past Life," "Towards Break of Day," "Easter 1916," copyright 1924 by
Macmillan Publishing Co., Inc., renewed 1952 by Bertha Georgie Yeats;
"Memory," "Phases of the Moon," copyright 1919 by Macmillan Publishing
Co., Inc., renewed 1947 by Bertha Georgie Yeats; "The Lover Pleads with His
Friends for Old Friends," "He Hears the Cry of the Sedge," copyright 1906 by
Macmillan Publishing Co., Inc., renewed 1934 by William Butler Yeats; re-
printed by permission of Macmillan Publishing Co., Inc., M. B. Yeats, Miss
Anne Yeats, and the Macmillan Co. of London and Basingstoke.

Portions of this book, in their original form, were first published in
Contemporary Literature, ELH, Mosaic, and *Paideuma.*

Printed in the United States of America

—for David H. Rosenthal

Knowledge the shade of a shade,
Yet must thou sail after knowledge

Canto 47

Foreword

Poetry is an art, and this book is about three artists. I have tried to read them anew, with a fresh eye and ear, while thinking about their presence for us now. Whatever life Yeats, Pound, and Eliot have for us comes through their poems—in the language of the poems themselves, through the centers of intensity to be found in them, in the balances of feeling and awareness their structures reveal.

These three men helped make a new world of poetry. They came to realize they were sailing into the unknown, in an apocalyptic era, on seas only partially charted by earlier masters and a few revolutionary thinkers. All three brought into the foreground of their practice the implicitly presentative and improvisatory character of poetry. All had their weaknesses as poets, and sometimes marred their work through a tendentiousness that could be obnoxious. Yet they remain great poets, not least because they contributed mightily to a new genre, the modern poetic sequence—fruit of more than a century of evolution and the crowning achievement of their individual careers.

Their continuing presence is further attested by the work of younger poets infected by their sensibilities and instructed by their formal discoveries. In my final chapter I suggest some of these continuities, which are simply the normal communion of poet with poet. Perhaps Victor Hugo was melodramatic when he called criticism "the adventure of the soul among masterpieces." He was thinking as an artist among works of art. His word "adventure" implies that a critic is journeying, at risk, into the unknown realm where fantasy and keenest observation and volatile emotions unite to create a reality of a thousand dimensions. All who embark on such voyages may chance upon a wonder or two before they return.

Yeats, Pound, and Eliot have, on the whole, been luckier than not in their scholars and critics. I have learned from many of them, with gratitude, despite having to insist that the independent life of a work of art is not to be made secondary to critical terminology or scholarly tracings. The stress must lie elsewhere if the passion and delight and serious play of poems are at all to be glimpsed in their own unique nature.

I first planned this voyage a number of years ago. Other enterprises intervened, and now it seems to me they were needed to help me clarify and simplify my purpose. I am grateful to all who have encouraged me by their sympathy, to which Victoria Rosenthal has added forbearance and Sally M. Gall a quizzical eye.

M. L. R.

Suffern, New York
May 1977

Contents

PART I

WHO ARE "YEATS, POUND, AND ELIOT"?

Chapter 1

The Poets Are Their Poems

What does it mean for a dead poet to be a living presence? In Book X of the *Odyssey* Circe tells Odysseus he must seek out the prophet Tiresias "who even dead, yet hath his mind entire" (Ezra Pound's translation, in Canto 47). Odysseus, since he existed in that land of myth where no flesh has trod, sailed forth, performed the necessary ritual, fed sacrificial blood to Tiresias, and held converse with the amazed, momentarily reincarnated sage.

But *we*, since we no longer hold with ritual sacrifice or bed with goddesses who tell us just where to go to receive revelation, must do as Pound did with Homer. Whether the poet be literally living or dead, we must open ourselves to possession by his "mind entire." I have been turning the thought around and around that the work of the great poets, who speak the most strikingly to our condition and can dazzle us with the music of their deepest awareness, remains virtually unknown. For most readers a few titles at best remain attached to certain names. One obvious reason is that, because of its

contradictory functions, language is the most demanding
of the plastic media available to artists—the most deceptive for the artist himself, the most tyrannical for his audience. We each live within a web of language adapted
at once to our separate, inner dreams and personalities
and to our outward daily lives. A poem of any energy insists on its own linguistic priority. It displaces, even
replaces, the system of language we ordinarily inhabit
and can send us far away indeed from our usual haunts
of consciousness:

> Who even dead, yet hath his mind entire!
> This sound came in the dark
> First must thou go the road
>   to hell . . .
> Ere thou come to thy road's end.

It is another's mind that takes us over; in a sense, it
will never leave the nervous system it has once invaded.
But when the fever, as it were, is past, a kind of forgetting does take place. Our usual world of language, never
forgotten, just in abeyance, resumes itself once more.
The alien was able to possess us for its prolonged moment, though, because it held us by its intensity as an
actor might do who with a gesture made the reality of
the character he was playing our own. In that moment of
submission to another sensibility, we share an emotional
world at once ours and outside ourselves: "transcendence." Yet even if the one poem becomes part of our
own experience forever, it does not speak for the poet's
other work. And so it happens that, at best, only a hand-
ful of pieces are familiar presences in most readers'
minds. The rest will be silence or something close to it, a
low indistinct susurrus in the middle distance. Part of
oneself prefers things to be that way. The invitation may

be, as it was to Odysseus, to "go the road / to hell" together with the poet.

Empathy is all. The presence, the *virtue*, waits openly in the poems themselves. It is there for us, whenever we are ready to go the road with it. And secondarily, it also sustains itself in those rarest readers who experience it rather than merely taking note and "appreciating." Among these readers the foremost are other poets, usually of a younger generation. The relationship of significant influence is of communion, even seduction: the irresistible insinuation of rhythm and idiom, of a distinctive voice in a state of arousal—inextinguishable flickerings of poetic continuity.

Who then are "Yeats, Pound, and Eliot"? Our short answer must be: their poems, in themselves and as they touch the work of others. Yes, the names belong to men who were once alive. But after each death we realized anew that, as Auden wrote of Yeats, "the death of the poet was kept from his poems." For the naked poem on the page neither the glamour of reputation nor the blankness of neglect counts. Here are three figures who in their ways have been the great progenitors of modern poetry in English—staples of literary history, objects of ideological praise and invective, mines and minefields for scholars and critics. We cannot in practice completely wave aside such considerations. If however we clear the way within ourselves as best we can, perhaps we shall hear the voices and catch the whole volatile movement of the poems of these men as vividly as possible.

In all this I mean nothing precious, nothing removed from the intimacy of life and society as we know them moment by moment. On the contrary, to hear a poem purely is to be privy to a verbally concentrated sharing of human intimacy, perfumed or rank, without interference from external "information." Take Eliot's little-known poem, "Lines for an Old Man":

> The tiger in the tiger-pit
> Is not more irritable than I.
> The whipping tail is not more still
> Than when I smell the enemy
> Writhing in the essential blood
> Or dangling from the friendly tree.
> When I lay bare the tooth of wit
> The hissing over the archéd tongue
> Is more affectionate than hate,
> More bitter than the love of youth,
> And inaccessible by the young.
> Reflected from my golden eye
> The dullard knows that he is mad.
> Tell me if I am not glad!

This poem exudes a *rank* odor of aging tiger in its description of an old man's passionate state, said to be beyond what the fiercest carnivore or the most excited and frustrated young person could feel. According to the title, the lines are not *by* an old man but *for* him to say. Eliot himself was in his mid-forties when he wrote the poem, whose extreme exacerbation is a form of hostile, self-loathing ecstasy. We can speculate that Eliot is hinting, with a sort of fearful gloating, at how old age will feel to him; or perhaps (and this is more likely) he feels that the state of mind he is experiencing is more appropriate for an old man than for him; or he may even simply be reflecting the attitude of old people he has observed. But none of this speculation is of any importance. The only thing that counts is the way this poem moves in the lines that are given us. First we see the "whipping," menacing, bloodthirsty tiger-image of the first five lines, keyed by the words "irritable" and "smell the enemy" especially. There is a sense in which the predator loves his victim, and that sense is carried over in the next five lines to the supposed old man's attitude toward those he wounds with his sarcasm and malice. The final three lines continue the tiger analogy with their central image of "my golden eye," in whose reflecting glow "dullards" see themselves to be "mad"—their dim rationality intensified in that sardonic mirror to something like frenzy. The exclamation in the very last line—"Tell me if I am not glad!"—assimilates that intensity to the speaker. His words there suggest, as so much of the phrasing in the poem does, that the state of feeling he describes is not purely negative. It has qualities of "affection," "love," "gladness." The emotion of the whole poem is uneasily complex, a confusion of motives fused in a sort of hellish, not quite identifiable joy.

The lines are for an old man, most probably, because they reflect a projected state of awareness that has brought the speaker beyond simplicities of attitude. It is a state of transport, a voice of one grown visionary out of his impotent articulateness—he has more to say than the young can understand, something that makes ordinary dull folk feel they are in a mad world. He speaks in riddles, and yet the progression of feeling, the dynamics of the poem's movement, are perfectly clear.

Establishing a speaker, or axes of reference of some dramatic or narrative or logical sort, helps the poet get a poem moving at a certain pitch and key. But the release of the poem into flight means that the dynamics, the succession of affects in the several units of phrasing, become central. That is why Yeats argues, half whimsically and altogether poignantly in his "All Souls' Night," that only the dead can be pure listeners. They alone can open themselves, without mockery, to the extremes of volatil-

ity to which his musings carry him: "To where the
damned have howled away their hearts / And where the
blessed dance."

> I need some mind that, if the cannon sound
> From every quarter of the world, can stay
> Wound in mind's pondering
> As mummies in the mummy-cloth are wound;
> Because I have a marvellous thing to say,
> A certain marvellous thing
> None but the living mock,
> Though not for sober ear;
> It may be all that hear
> Should laugh and weep an hour upon the clock.

Being alive, we are of course at a certain disadvantage.
Still, can we not lay aside sobriety and mocking mettle-
someness long enough, on occasion, simply to open ourselves to whatever the language brings us? For instance,
both these passages I have quoted are extremely serious
and very witty, and sometimes downright comic, at one
and the same time. Yeats's observation that "none but
the living" will mock what he has to say is a joke, although the serious thought is also present that anyone
alive must think him silly for entertaining such fantasies
as he is about to express. Yeats employs a fey face-
tiousness here to induce openness to a weird, unstable
frame of mind. The ferocity of the "old man" speaking in
Eliot's poem approaches a similar state; its nearly comic
exaggeration masks a dead serious quarrel with both
death and life. In both poems, opposite states of feeling
are fused together. The fusion creates an atmosphere of
riddling mystery and of a barely controlled, unidentifiable pressure of feeling.

In the next three chapters, I shall follow each of our
poets into at least one of the poems he still inhabits with

mind entire, a sample generously characteristic of him.
Each of these poem-worlds is perforce alien to us because it is at once the discovery and the creation of an
original mind engaged with reality in its own way. Yet
each of them, too, is surprisingly recognizable, unfolding states of awareness always with us but in different
perspectives. I have already recalled how, at the start of
Canto 47, Pound recovers for us the world of Homer's
Odyssey. But in the act of so doing, he stamps the poem,
in a momentarily confusing opening line, with his own
obsessions and his own methods of poetic realization.

> Who even dead, yet hath his mind entire!
> This sound came in the dark
> First must thou go the road
>   to hell
> And to the bower of Ceres' daughter Proserpine,
> Through overhanging dark, to see Tiresias,
> Eyeless that was, a shade, that is in hell
> So full of knowing that the beefy men know less than he,
> Ere thou come to thy road's end.

In the more extended discussions to follow, I shall
begin with this poem for several reasons. Chief among
them is the fact that Canto 47 directly acts out that communion of past and present which, felt at the pitch of experience, is nothing less than our human meaning in
process. All three of our poets live at that pitch in their
work, but Pound (even more than Browning, from
whom he learned so much) is its keenest exemplar. What
is involved is the linguistic mobilization of memory and
knowledge as energy acting in the immediate present,
not as dead "information" about an inert past. We shall
see further into the process, I hope, in Chapters 3 and 4,
the former centered on Yeats's "Meditations in Time of
Civil War" and "Nineteen Hundred and Nineteen," the

latter on Eliot's "Little Gidding." With poetry that has
such tremendous power of evocation—of private and racial memory, of the relation of the secretly brooding self
to the world around it, and of elusive states of sensation
and reverie that are our truest self-confirmation—we
have only one thing to do: plunge into the poems and
see where they take us.

Throughout this book I have some general points to
make. For instance, there is Pound's intriguing adven-
turousness of method, as in his experiments with structure; and of course there is the matter of his political tendentiousness as it enters his poetry. All three of the
poets, indeed, have their own forms of tendentiousness.
If their work is a struggle for appropriate form by masters in the foreground of their art, that struggle is in part
an effort to relate their aesthetic to their sense of the
most crucial aspects of the human condition. Yeats's radically original use of conventional forms is an expression
of the struggle, and so is Eliot's balancing of a psychologically subtle modern sensibility, with an exquisite sense
of the absurd, against his will to affirm Christian faith.

But these general observations, and others concerning
these poets' practice and preoccupations, are incidental
to the idiosyncratic life and force of individual poems—
something to be explored one poem at a time, and again
and again. In that idiosyncratic life and force lie their
value and the essence of their relationship to younger
poets that I shall comment on in my final chapter. For
illustration, just look again, quickly, at the quotations on
the foregoing pages. Look at Eliot's improvisation, in
"Lines for an Old Man," of a modified sonnet in a sort of
syncopated tetrameter, with a nervously ragged yet persistent set of rhymes and half-rhymes culminating in the
delphic couplet at the end. Look at the extraordinary
ease and naturalness with which the stanza from Yeats's

"All Souls' Night" handles its more regular rhyme-scheme and its intricate dance of line-lengths while balancing formal and incantatory speech with intimate and colloquial phrasing. And in the lines from Pound's Canto 47, look at the use of slightly archaic diction to invoke chthonic mysteries as they impinge on the thinking mind; and at the intricate play of sound in which the invocation is enmeshed. One does not wish to labor such details, and yet one can no more ignore them than the poets themselves could. The virtuosity in all these instances goes far beyond the craftsmanship of lesser poetry. It is a mode of energy—of the intense discovery of a subjective state that has been pressing for realization in orchestrated phrasing. In short, it is the vitally inventive element that not only brings a poem to birth but also then persists as a continuing energy within it.

Chapter 2

Voyage of Sensibility:
POUND'S CANTO 47

The attentive reader will surely be struck by the subtleties of Pound's recasting of the Homeric text into modern poetic idiom. The opening lines of Canto 47 that I have quoted still present Odysseus speaking, but we no longer have a completely straightforward narrative. The very first line jolts our understanding deliberately. Unless we recognize the quotation at once, it looks at first like a riddle, one unaccountably couched in an exclamation rather than a question. Pound has lifted it out of its proper context, the description of Tiresias a few lines further along. And so this paradoxical outcry stays floating there at the start of the canto, portentous and waiting for its relevance to be made clear. Even the mysterious second line—"This sound came in the dark"—floats in place a little ambiguously and ominously, perhaps a reference to the opening line, perhaps to the lines that follow, perhaps to both. Plainer than the first line, it is nevertheless almost as ringing and riddling.

So the two initial musical phrases seem to enter arbitrarily and disconcertingly. But they settle into context as the succeeding lines emerge with perfect clarity. These lines project the primitive awe of Homer's text. The third and fourth lines drop us, with a lurch, into a vision of hell, and the deepened tone is sustained by occasional archaic diction and by a stock epithet ("beefy men") suggestive of traditional epic as well as by the long, prophetically incantatory sentence.

The passage as a whole is as much an experimental use of traditional materials as it is a reminder of their continuing magnetism and mystery. It is serious verbal play, or syntactic play. We have seen how it plucks a paradoxical note from its original context and gains extraordinary emphasis by the displacement. Read as a series of tonal notes, the passage begins with its riddling exclamation and then sustains the ominousness and mystification by the reverberating second line, "This sound came in the dark." In the echoing associations of these two lines a sort of equivalence exists between communication with the dead in Homer's mythic world and the invasion of dark psychic recesses by the repossessed mentality of a past age. Heightened alertness to the encroachments of death and darkness is a necessary condition of the sensitized awareness of this speaker, whose voice is a fusion of that of Odysseus and of a modern intelligence close to Pound's own.

What is the point of this reimprovisation of Homer? The whole glow of its movement comes from its entranced companionship with the older text, yet that companionship merely sets the poem on a further journey of awareness.

> Knowledge the shade of a shade,
> Yet must thou sail after knowledge
> Knowing less than the drugged beasts. *phtheggometha thasson*
> φθεγγώμεθα θᾶσσον

> The small lamps drift in the bay
> And the sea's claw gathers them.
> Neptunus drinks after neap-tide.

The opening displacements were a clue to the method further revealed here, where Homer is decisively subordinated to a modern sensibility. Homer's Odysseus was not a subjective man; Pound's isolation of the one paradoxical thought about Tiresias begins to make him so. It is this reconceived Odysseus who defines for himself a task at once virtually hopeless and yet irrevocable. Nor would Homer's Odysseus ever have called knowledge "the shade of a shade." Dante's and Tennyson's Odysseus (i.e., "Ulysses") might have pondered the matter, but not Homer's man. Such modern skepticism, and the Platonic sophistication underlying it, would have been thoroughly alien to him for all his wiliness. Nor would he have entertained the notion of a doomed voyage to seek out knowledge for its own sake—not that archaic pragmatist whose world was a perfect balance between absolute certainty and absolute terror! Similarly, what was for the Homeric Greeks a calculated risk under pressure—Polites' rallying cry at Circe's gate (*"phtheggometha thasson"*—"Let's give a shout right now!"*) becomes for Pound an image of leaping into the unknown for the sake of knowledge. Living dangerously on principle is the only alternative to remaining forever ignorant out of timidity, more ignorant even than Odysseus's companions after they were drugged by Circe and turned into beasts.

Like Odysseus, Pound guards against hubris. In the next three lines, beginning "The small lamps drift," he wards off any impression of it. We have the gentlest suggestion here that the small lamps in the bay are like men who "sail after knowledge." They are vulnerable to "the sea's claw" just as Odysseus was, and like him they are enduring and resistant despite their exposure as they are drawn, smoothly at first, out into potentially violent seas. Traditionally they symbolize the souls of the dead setting out into the unknown chaos beyond life, and in the West they are often associated with All Souls' Night. Pound converts the symbolism into a suggestion of his own poetic enterprise as well as of Odysseus's perilous adventure: associations of vulnerability and courage rather than power.

Canto 47, then, reenacts Homer's Book X but does so by planting Odyssean moments amid disjunct passages of varying tones and intensities. It thus shifts attention from the traditional, myth-based epic to the workings of an alert, subjective modern sensibility completely at home with the older work and to an important degree obsessed by it. The *Odyssey* becomes a set of points of reference for that sensibility, one end of a scale that, at the other end, extends to the intimate psyche of the modern speaker. The canto moves through phases of feeling and awareness that depend on the Homeric narrative in that they *occupy* it. At the same time, they dismantle its structure and redistribute the components according to the needs of the speaking sensibility that plays the role of Odysseus *redivivus.* We could hardly have a more beautiful instance of poetic repossession and reawakening of the significant past.

The process began, as we have seen, with the two opening lines, whose mysterious and ominous resonance holds sway even after the immediately succeeding lines firmly anchor them in their proper original context. Then, in the passage last quoted, more non-Homeric notes are introduced. In the next stage, even the clearly Odyssean associations grow unexpectedly intense and centrifugal.

Neptunus drinks after neap-tide.
Tamuz! Tamuz!!
The red flame going seaward.
            By this gate art thou measured.
From the long boats they have set lights in the water,
The sea's claw gathers them outward.
Scilla's dogs snarl at the cliff's base,
The white teeth gnaw in under the crag,
But in the pale night the small lamps float seaward
                    Τυ Διώνα
                    TU DIONA
Και Μοῖραι᾽ ῾Άδονιν
Kai MOIRAI᾽ ADONIN
The sea is streaked red with Adonis,
The lights flicker red in small jars.
Wheat shoots rise new by the altar,
            flower from the swift seed.
Two span, two span to a woman,
Beyond that she believes not. Nothing is of any importance.
To that is she bent, her intention
To that art thou called ever turning intention . . .

   The rapidly accumulating associations and images here are only tangentially relevant to the *Odyssey*. Once the presence of the older work had been established (something that happened at the very start of *The Cantos*), it became a subordinate if highly important aspect of the speaker's consciousness. Sometimes the speaker adds images of his own even when the immediate context is Homeric, as in the alliterative line "Neptunus drinks after neap-tide." Pound's addition suggests hyperanimality as one attribute of the god, who awaits the optimum time to drink deep of the sea. Moreover, Homer did not of course use the Latin name of Poseidon, Odysseus's great enemy. Pound *uses* Homer rather than merely rendering him. The echoing sounds of "Neptunus" and "neap-tide" were reasons enough for the shift; but in addition Pound casts a wide net of multiple cultural and mythological association, and "Neptunus" gives us a Roman dimension. Similarly, Homer does not speak of Tammuz, the Babylonian equivalent of Adonis. Yet Pound introduces him and, for good measure, follows his name with double exclamation points to stress the extended association.

In short, the speaker has occupied his symbol: Odysseus in the context of Homeric consciousness and of mythical consciousness generally. He has grafted the persona of Odysseus onto himself. Thus Pound brings his interest in comparative religion directly into the poem. The archaic image of Odysseus becomes a living mask of the sophisticated Pound in such a way that the original Homeric context merges with a twentieth-century awareness of myth and ritual. Hence the whole body of lore concerning phallic vegetation gods and their earth-mother counterparts—Adonis and Tammuz, Dione and Aphrodite—enters the poem. (Canto 47 was published in 1937, twenty-two years after the final volume appeared of Sir James Frazer's *The Golden Bough*.) Odysseus's sexual knowledge of Circe and other goddesses, and of Penelope in their bed carved out of the living tree, becomes part of that lore. So does the speaker himself. At the center of the poem's consciousness, the poet is an Odysseus of the modern imagination and the ultimate embodiment of the male creative principle. He cannot help penetrating the female principle of responsive, malleable reality that actively compels the direction of his power.

The poem itself is nevertheless something other than all this explanation. Its immediacies of image, tone, and rhythm simply present realization in action, in a world simultaneously empirical and mythical but never abstract. The speaker is at once Pound himself and Odys-

seus and Tammuz-Adonis. He is lying with a real
woman who is also the fertility goddess (Circe-Dione-
Aphrodite) imperiously intent on being impregnated.
"The stars are not in her counting, / To her they are but
wandering holes. / Begin thy plowing." The darkness in
which they are lying is the breeding place of the unknown. The depths of Erebus and of inescapable sexuality, and the mythical figures with which the speaker's
mind teems, are all aspects of his own human situation,
his range of awareness that is the poem's given reality.

The thou who is addressed (and who becomes "I" in
the closing stanza) is summoned by "she"—the female
darkness. He must embark on the self-obliterating, sacrificial voyage into death of his old self and toward rebirth: "By this gate art thou measured." In visualizing
this destiny, the poem elaborates on the images of terror
always present in the *Odyssey* (Scylla and Charybdis, for
example) but also introduces multiple associations from
the Adonis-Aphrodite mythology. The line "The sea is
streaked red with Adonis" is a perfect instance. Its clear
evocation is of bloody death associated with the very nature of the hero who "sails after knowledge." Earlier
images—"the small lamps drift in the bay," "the sea's
claw," "the red flame going seaward"—have built into
this one. I have mentioned only a few elements in an intricate lacework of suggestion that culminates, in the
passage beginning "Neptunus drinks after neap-tide,"
in the elegiac words from Bion's "Lament for Adonis"—
"*Kai* MOIRAI' ADONIN" ("And the fates [weep for]
Adonis")—and in the line that refers explicitly to the
blood of Adonis.

It is interesting that the first line in the poem ("Who
even dead, yet hath his mind entire!") refers to Tiresias,
yet carries over to the slain hero-god who will be reborn
and to the modern speaker in whom the "dead" experi-

ence of the past reawakens. An analogy with musical structure will help show how the poem works. Each effect is self-contained but flows into and is picked up by other effects, and each is clear in itself even while it builds into a larger pattern of tonal exploration. The poem begins in dark, death-involved mystery and terror, strong with the sense of personal doom; it quickly introduces a mood of desolate resolution, sustained by the strangeness and hardness of a new set of images constructed around Tammuz-Adonis and the "small lamps" and the hostile sea. Then, with "Wheat shoots rise new by the altar," a second large tonal movement, in a new key, enters the poem brilliantly.

The shift of key in the new movement is modulated by the persistence of a fatalistic tone despite the emphasis now on the fructifying sexual act. To plunge into the charged, fecund darkness is the hero's dangerous, unavoidable task, an engagement with impersonal destiny in an impossible if irresistible private struggle. The result is the triumph of the life principle at the expense of individuality—the most delightful of disasters, no doubt, but something very different from sheer voluptuous joy. In the mythology the hero dies in the process—"Wheat shoots rise new by the altar," but the price is that "the sea is streaked red with Adonis." And as we have seen in lines already quoted, the female principle is not so much seductive as magnetically controlling—

Two span, two span to a woman,
Beyond that she believes not. Nothing is of any importance.
To that is she bent, her intention
To that art thou called ever turning intention . . .

These lines give one example among many of Pound's extraordinary craftsmanship. His compulsive repetitions

(like D. H. Lawrence's in comparable moments of realization) and sound-echoings act out the experience of
impassioned subjection of one's will. The internal
rhymes and half-rhymes and consonance are enormously
effective in this emotional context: "span," "woman,"
"beyond," "any," "importance," "bent," "intention"—
particularly the last two. Nor is it fanciful to note that the
passage creates a special implied stress (though not in
the actual pronunciation) on the prefix *in-* in "intention"
as if a coined word, *"in-*tension," were also present. As
with "bent," there is a play here on the ideas of "purpose" and of "tension." Further along, this absorption
with the ceaseless sexuality of nature and our helpless
participation in it evolves a culminating passage that is
one of the triumphs of modern lyric poetry.

> And the small stars now fall from the olive branch,
> Forked shadow falls dark on the terrace
> More black than the floating martin
>   that has no care for your presence,
> His wing-print is black on the roof tiles
> And the print is gone with his cry.
> So light is thy weight on Tellus
> Thy notch no deeper indented
> Thy weight less than the shadow
> Yet hast thou gnawed through the mountain,
>   Scylla's white teeth less sharp.
> Hast thou found a nest softer than cunnus
> Or hast thou found better rest
> Hast'ou a deeper planting, doth thy death year
> Bring swifter shoot?
> Hast thou entered more deeply the mountain?

These lovely images sustain much of the earlier paradoxical melancholy, the sense of being carried into oblivion by one's fatal potency. But the delicacy of the opening lines and the erotic fullness of the five closing ones, as well as the godlike conception of being Tellus's lover, change the proportions of feeling. The rhetorical question "Hast thou found a nest softer than cunnus?" is exultant, even if asked of Dionysus himself in the full knowledge that he must die in the service of cosmic procreation. The passage finds a perfect metaphor, precise and sympathetic, for the insignificance of all individual achievement—"So light is thy weight on Tellus / Thy notch no deeper indented / Thy weight less than the shadow." At the same time it insists that male creative power does nevertheless prevail. Two sides of heroic experience are balanced here. Part of that experience is to learn how minimal is the effect of one's efforts. The other part is to see that the effort must nevertheless be made and that it will have its successes after all: "Yet hast thou gnawed through the mountain, / Scylla's white teeth less sharp."

The movement from lightly falling or floating sense-impressions, at once disappearing and incisive, to utterly rich possession by the softness of "cunnus" and then to imagery of deep-thrusting sexual power condenses and epitomizes the consciousness of the canto in all its aspects. The remainder of the canto takes its falling energy from this curve of movement. That is, it mingles notes of ripe flourishing with death-notes. "Adonis falleth. / Fruit cometh after. The small lights drift out with the tide." The curve is plotted, almost, along points of imagery that are at once independent of literal sexual reference and sexually suggestive—"Forked shadow falls," for instance, or "Thy notch no deeper indented," or "a deeper planting." It is not a matter of haranguing us but of carrying us along a complex network of awareness that is in effect a system of sensitized encompassment.

This last consideration brings me to one final observation among the many that fuller attention to the canto would demand. It is the use of the word "Molü" (usually spelled "Moly" in transliteration from the Greek). The word occurs at the end of the "two span, two span to a woman" passage whose beginning I have quoted and discussed. The longer passage reads:

Two span, two span to a woman,
Beyond that she believes not. Nothing is of any importance.
To that is she bent, her intention
To that art thou called ever turning intention,
Whether by night the owl-call, whether by sap in shoot,
Never idle, by no means by no wiles intermittent
Moth is called over mountain
The bull runs blind on the sword, *naturans*
To the cave art thou called, Odysseus,
By Molü hast thou respite for a little,
By Molü art thou freed from the one bed
        that thou may'st return to another

Literally, we remember, Molü was the magical herb that Hermes gave Odysseus to keep him from being turned into a beast by Circe's magic. Simple symbolic conversion, such as we normally avoid unless the text itself pushes us into it, would translate Molü into a gift of spiritual and intellectual power over our grosser tendencies. This interpretation would provide a "rational" explanation to nonpuritanical readers of how the hero became the goddess's lover without being reduced by her to abject bestiality. I mention all this because Pound, after referring to Molü in the sense of its literal use by Odysseus in the foregoing passage, alludes to it again, differently, in the two lines that close the canto:

        that hath the gift of healing,
    that hath the power over wild beasts.

Here the spiritual meaning of Molü is obviously intended, and also a further meaning: the power of the remembering and transcendent imagination. It is the artistic equivalent of the heroic and sexual mission of
Odysseus, and it puts in unsentimental yet emotionally
reassuring perspective the relation of human genius to
the irresistible, nonhuman force of natural process. This
is the "knowledge" spoken of earlier, toward which the
entire canto has "sailed."

Yeats seems to me the greatest poet in English of the
century, and yet the spell of Canto 47 is such that for the
moment I find it impossible to think of a poem of his
that quite matches it. I know I have only to launch myself Yeats-wards, into a poem like "Sailing to Byzantium" or "News for the Delphic Oracle" (both of which
have preoccupations in common with Canto 47), and
soon enough I will be caught up in its orbit. But the hold
of a superb poem one has just been giving oneself to is
negative as well as positive; that is, it tends to detach us
from other works toward which we have felt an affinity.

The authority of Canto 47 is related to its fused tradi-
tionalism and modernity. Despite the archaic diction
with which it conjures up the vitality of myth and incantation in the past, the poem is harshly intelligent and
unsentimental. Its fatalism cuts sharply against its own
insistence on the redeeming power, however shortlived,
of courageous imaginative awareness. The open, associative form gives an impression of rigor rather than
looseness, of an inner coherence in the highly charged
dynamics. The poem's complex volatility would certainly
have bogged it down had Pound tried more conventional
modes of poetic exposition and narration, or even of
stanza-form. Ideas in this poem are not superimposed
but are an aspect of its conceptual energy. In a poem like

this one, the speaker's initial positioning is very different from that in a characteristic poem by Yeats. The process is already fully under way at the start. It is up to us—we are given clues aplenty in the successive units of phrasing—to let it draw us into its developing context. Vibrant nodules mark the way as the process tentatively completes itself.

Now Yeats, too, often begins a poem in the middle of things, but very much more in the manner of one of Browning's dramatic monologues or one of Keats's odes. He presents a speaker looking at a scene or situation, so that we have as it were a static moment of placement, a setting of the stage or focusing of the relationship between the speaker and the object of his attention. "That is no country for old men," says the old man who speaks in "Sailing to Byzantium." And then we are off into the speaker's predicament of exclusion from "that country," the country of youth and procreation, and the way in which he will deal with the predicament (for even the aged poet-hero needs his appropriate kind of Molü). Thus begins the volume called *The Tower*, in which Yeats reached his full maturity. "Sailing to Byzantium" is followed by the title-poem, which again starts out by posing an issue—in fact the same issue, introduced this time with an almost embarrassing outcry:

> What shall I do with this absurdity—
> O heart, O troubled heart—this caricature,
> Decrepit age that has been tied to me
> As to a dog's tail?

Compare these lines with the opening of Canto 47—"Who even dead, yet hath his mind entire!" One can see Pound's appeal to the schools of "post-modernism" that have tried to get out from under what they consider the burden of subjectivity. Their avowed aim is to subordinate the poem's movement to objective process—that is, to have the thinking mind of the poem take its cues from wherever it is at a given moment in the midst of swirling or stagnant reality. The connection with Pound's method is that Pound expects the reader to locate the specific context from the process of the poem itself. There is, though, an important difference in the two positions. Although they are challenging and suggestive, the "post-modernist" writers—Charles Olson, for example—actually indulge in subjectivity far more than do the older masters who are sometimes called "ego-centered." The explorations of a Pound or a Yeats are after all serious efforts to place their objectified awareness in a purview beyond the merely personal. On the other hand, submitting one's art to undifferentiated process is a kind of random videotaping. What other aim can it have than to confirm one's presence, mainly as a complaisant recorder, in the indifferent universe? It is voting for entropy with a vengeance. But that is a subject to be dealt with farther down the line. Meanwhile, there is an important sense in which none of this sort of thinking matters a bit. That sense takes charge once one turns from literary "positions" to actual poems. Somehow the "positions" do have a relationship to the way poets write and readers read and critics criticize, but it all seems far away from the place where the real poem, of any school, lives. How can we do anything else but attend when the authentic voice and music catch our attention? What they bring us is like

> the floating martin
> that has no care for your presence,
> His wing-print is black on the roof tiles
> And the print is gone with his cry.

Chapter 3

Structure and Process:
YEATS'S CIVIL WAR SEQUENCES

In this matter of structure and process, as in other central respects, it is interesting to compare Pound's Canto 47 with Yeats's companion-sequences that follow hard upon the opening poems of *The Tower* I have already mentioned. These sequences are "Meditations in Time of Civil War" and "Nineteen Hundred and Nineteen," groups of seven and six poems respectively.

The differences are very obvious. Yeats does not hold worlds of psychic cross-reference in volatile solution as Pound does. He does not play with tones and voices as units of pure affect with Pound's abandon. Nor is he as glancingly allusive; he builds his context into his poems more solidly and explicitly, at least on the surface. Yet he too works simultaneously with multiple points of reference, creating small poetic systems: sequences with many characteristics of a lyric poem writ large. If the word "simultaneously" seems odd here, one must remember that any two or more effects in a single work of art coexist within the completed work. Because literature, like music and dance, unfolds over a period of time as one goes from beginning to end, one must wait out the first experience of a whole work to see how this is so. Pound's own great lifework was his enormous would-be sequence *The Cantos,* but as we shall see it is vastly different from Yeats's more tightly contained structures.

Let me very quickly review the nature of the modern poetic sequence. It is both our characteristic form of the long poem and the outstanding development, going back at least as far as Whitman, in our poetry for over a century. Intimate, fragmented, open, and emotionally volatile, it meets the needs of modern sensibility so naturally that its evolution has gone all but unnoticed. Ordinarily it consists of a grouping of mainly lyric poems and passages, rarely uniform in pattern, that tend to interact as an organic whole. It usually includes narrative, dramatic, and ratiocinative elements, but its ordering is finally lyrical, a succession of *affects*—that is, of units of phrasing that generate specific intensities of feeling and states of awareness. Because of these separate radiating centers, the sequence meets Poe's significantly modern objection to the idea of a long poem: namely, that it is impossible because of the limited duration of any one surge of emotional energy.

In addition, the sequence is openly improvisational and tentative in structure, a condition in fact of all art but often papered over by the conventions of set forms. It would certainly not be very difficult, for instance, to see Browning's *Sordello* in this light. Indeed, Browning often goes to great lengths to escape the tyranny of conventional expectations of continuity. And Tennyson's *Maud* is very nearly a sequence, for its neurotically sensitive protagonist exists, poetically speaking, to give the author an excuse for juxtaposing extremely different emotional states—a dramatic justification for arranging a sequence of affects in dynamically effective order.

Maud is especially interesting as a precursor because the characteristic voice of a sequence operates under pressure. Sometimes the speaker is *in extremis.* More often he or she is oppressed by what Delmore Schwartz called "the burden of consciousness," locked in Laocoön-like struggle with a moribund yet murderous civilization. Seeking to objectify itself, the speaking sensibility calls up sunken dimensions of its consciousness from the depths, moving through confusions and ambiguities toward a precarious balance. The process is as much cultural as psychological. The heroic or tragic aspect of the sequence lies in its protagonist's effort to pit personal, historical, and artistic memory or vision against anomie and alienation. In short, the modern poetic sequence has evolved out of a serious need for a poetry even more encompassing than even the greatest single lyric poem. It hardly needs saying that in examining Pound's Canto 47 we have already begun to engage ourselves with a *locus classicus* of the genre: *The Cantos,* to which we shall return in a later chapter. At this point, however, I wish to look at two interrelated sequences by Yeats that are simpler and shorter than *The Cantos.*

Yeats's "Nineteen Hundred and Nineteen" was written the year of its title and published two years later. "Meditations in Time of Civil War" was written in 1923 and published in 1924. When Yeats included them both in his volume *The Tower* (1928), he placed them together but in the reverse order of their composition. From their titles alone one can see that he composed them under the pressure of political events, and if one reads through the thirteen poems that comprise them their reciprocity is clear—they are a single constellation, or twin-sequence.

The immediate context of "Meditations," which is the more concretely personal and local of the two, is postwar Ireland during the "troubles." That of "Nineteen Hundred and Nineteen" is the whole turbulence of modern history during the Great War and just after. (An earlier title, in fact, was "Thoughts upon the Present State of the World.") Once the sequences were reversed in order, the second seemed to take off naturally from the first into its more encompassing orbit of passionately tragic vision. One would surely have thought that Yeats had written them that way from the start. I can only conjecture that the surging dismay, and the consciousness of his spiritual isolation amidst vicious savagery, in "Nineteen Hundred and Nineteen" came readily to Yeats by 1919. He had already written poems like "Easter 1916" and the various pieces in *Responsibilities* and elsewhere that foreshadow the clear-eyed disillusionment and bitter Romantic energy of that sequence. But he needed more time to reach back to the particular circumstances and experiences in his own life that lay behind his acute personal sense of historical disaster: the materials out of which he constructed "Meditations in Time of Civil War."

In any case, once he had completed the sequences and reversed their order, the dynamics of their movement seemed inevitable. Taken singly, the poems in them are more traditionally structured, more "old-fashioned," than Canto 47. In combination, they take on a complex simultaneity like that of Pound's poem, an organic body of awareness of the tidal flow of feeling that is the subjective undertow of history. The speaker is at once caught up in the world he is observing and apart from it, staring transfixed at an apocalyptic moment in the cyclical rise and fall of civilizations. "Meditations" opens ironically with a comment on the helpless abdication of responsibility by the traditional gentry, contrary to all surface appearances:

> Surely among a rich man's flowering lawns,
> Amid the rustle of his planted hills,
> Life overflows without ambitious pains;
> And rains down life until the basin spills,
> And mounts more dizzy high the more it rains
> As though to choose whatever shape it wills
> And never stoop to a mechanical
> Or servile shape, at others' beck and call.
>
> Mere dreams, mere dreams! . . .

The rise in intensity between this poem, "Ancestral Houses," which sets the "Meditations" going, and the nightmare vision of history at the end of "Nineteen Hundred and Nineteen" marks the main curve of movement in the double sequence. The movement completes itself in the archetypal images of recurrent terror that appear in the final poem, which begins:

> Violence upon the roads: violence of horses;
> Some few have handsome riders, are garlanded
> On delicate sensitive ear or tossing mane,
> But wearied running round and round in their courses
> All break and vanish, and evil gathers head:
> Herodias' daughters have returned again,
> A sudden blast of dusty wind and after
> Thunder of feet, tumult of images,
> Their purpose in the labyrinth of the wind . . .

In between "Ancestral Houses" and Poem VI of "Nineteen Hundred and Nineteen" (whose individual poems are untitled) the movement has three major phases. "Ancestral Houses" is a wry overture on the many-sided theme of the brutal discrepancy between reality and dream on which all the poems play. In its relatively

low-keyed way it opens us to the stronger music to follow. The rest of "Meditations" then takes us through the
first two phases in the major movement of the sequences. The first brings us into the poet's self-enclosed
fantasy of creating anew, in his own home and family,
the obsolete realm of aristocratic dedication forgotten by
his country's great families. The second shows the crushing of that fantasy by the violence of history. The third
phase is developed in the whole of "Nineteen Hundred
and Nineteen," a complex little structure in itself. Poem I
recapitulates the emotional discovery of "Meditation,"
but at a stormier and more cosmic level, and the remaining five poems relate this state of awareness to a number
of others—particularly to the ultimate image of the "solitary" individual human soul as a swan that "has leaped
into the desolate heaven."

This image appears in Poem III, the point of deepest
internalization of all the motifs of the twin-sequence into
the dreaming knowledge of the speaking self. Man seeks
to re-create himself socially through politics, and per-
sonally through art, and in both instances comes up
against the intransigence of impersonal process. Such is
the bearing of the symbolic argument presented in Poem
III—but the language and spirit are of a magnificent,
doomed adventure like the Odyssean one of Canto 47.
The brief gleam of soul's life in Yeats's lines parallels the
glimmering of the small lamps setting forth, and the im-
permanent power of Molü, in Pound's poem.

> Some moralist or mythological poet
> Compares the solitary soul to a swan;
> I am satisfied with that,
> Satisfied if a troubled mirror show it,
> Before that brief gleam of its life be gone,
> An image of its state;
> The wings half spread for flight,

The breast thrust out in pride
Whether to play, or to ride
Those winds that clamour of approaching night.

A man in his own secret meditation
Is lost amid the labyrinth that he has made
In art or politics;
Some Platonist affirms that in the station
Where we should cast off body and trade
The ancient habit sticks,
And that if our works could
But vanish with our breath
That were a lucky death,
For triumph can but mar our solitude.

The swan has leaped into the desolate heaven:
That image can bring wildness, bring a rage
To end all things, to end
What my laborious life imagined, even
The half-imagined, the half-written page . . .

The state of balance reached here compresses within a few lines the main oppositions of both sequences, from the furthest reach of the most daring dreams to the most fumbling sense of personal inadequacy. The idea that any illusion of fixing reality in a perfect form diverts the soul's attention from its true state—an impossible readiness for potentiality amidst utter objective chaos—is itself an oxymoron identifying mature wisdom with introvert withdrawal. Yeats had put the matter less philosophically and glamorously in the down-to-earth explanation of his own nature at the close of "Meditations":

The abstract joy,
The half-read wisdom of daemonic images,
Suffice the ageing man as once the growing boy.

But it is toward the balance of Poem III and then around it that the sequences move—toward the state in which, though the word "triumph" can still be used, it is valued less than the precious solitude of the human soul face to face with mutability and death.

I have suggested that the first stage of this movement comes in "Meditations," after "Ancestral Houses" has prepared the way. In a group of three serious yet whimsically eccentric poems, "My House," "My Table," and "My Descendants," Yeats talks of his country home in an old Norman tower and imagines that he and his family have somehow taken over the role of the failed aristocracy. Their form of *noblesse* will be a fusion of simplicity, aestheticism, high meditation, and what he elsewhere calls "the ceremony of innocence." "My Table," for instance, is focused on a samurai sword in the poet's study. To him it speaks with silent eloquence of heroic family traditions and of a mystical link between one's love of beautiful craftsmanship and one's moral élan— the right to "pass Heaven's door." "My Table," with its succession of rhyming couplets in a single unbroken stanza, is the most urgently incantatory of these opening poems. The speaker is willing himself into the exalted mentality of a forgotten time and an exotic culture, an idealized ancient Japan where art and beauty, élite responsibility, and religious duty were one. The sword is an emblem of the violent world of the past whose need to be transformed into its opposite led to such ideals; as an aesthetic object it embodies the opposite condition as well.

Here I must go back for a moment to "Ancestral Houses." It provided a dark opening for the first movement, and its initial acidly elegiac tonalities are intimately bound up with the lyrical development of the motif of failed dreams in all the poems. The passage ("Surely among a rich man's . . .") already quoted ends with the outcry "Mere dreams, mere dreams!" Indeed, what is striking about this poem is not so much its specific theme; most of us, after all, have never had any illusions about the virtues of "great" families. But that outcry, and the atmosphere of bleak disappointment that goes with it and with the poem's repeated ironies toward the present masters of "ancestral houses," gives us the first, most crucial context for the word "dreams" among the many in the twin-sequence. The irony is especially strong in the poem's use of the term "rich man" to degrade the contemporary aristocracy. Homer's genius, the poem goes on to say, was inspired by a genuinely aristocratic spirit, the "abounding glittering jet." But our modern experience imposes a changed metaphor; for us there is only a "marvellous empty sea-shell," separated from its sources that lie in "the obscure dark of rich streams." This last image, symbolic of the psyche itself, implies that we must re-create our meanings anew from the mysterious springs in racial memory. "Bitter and violent" founders of great lines in the past, we are told, created the dream of beauty and civilization because unhappy with their own lives. They commanded artists and architects to

> rear in stone
> The sweetness that all longed for night and day,
> The gentleness none there had ever known . . .

All those bitter, violent founders were like the samurai whose passion and discipline "My Table" exalts in the emblem of the beautiful sword. "Ancestral Houses" clearly implies that only artists themselves in their vision-haunted intensity can now summon the will and imagination to live for such dreams. The three poems that follow—"My House," "My Table," and "My Descendants"—act out this role. "My House" shows the poet as the true aristocratic inheritor, laboring in his tower like *"Il Penseroso's* Platonist"* to conjure up visions of the "sweetness" and "gentleness"—transcendent joy and knowledge. The allusion is to the passage in which Milton imagines himself, similarly inspired,

> in some high lonely Tower,
> Where I may oft out-watch the *Bear,*
> With thrice great Hermes, or unsphear
> The spirit of *Plato* to unfold
> What worlds, or what vast regions . . .

In "My House" and "My Table" Yeats successively dons two masks of visionary wholeness from the past, that of Milton's "Platonist" and that of the Japanese warrior-aesthete. He does so only partially, for it is more a matter of summoning up their worlds than actually calling himself Milton or a samurai; and so Yeats does not go as far as Pound goes when he actually does become Odysseus *redivivus.* Still, Yeats's imagination is similarly reaching into an alternative state of being to his own literal self. Having gone so far out of himself, as it were, he grows gentler and more humanly familiar in "My Descendants." This poem shows him at his most exposed and personal in these four opening poems— quietly happy despite the pomposity of the first two stanzas, in which his aristocratic play-acting grows solemnly egotistical for the moment. Both tones, the pompous and the intimately relaxed, are appropriate before the sledgehammer blow falls of the next poem, "The Road at My Door." When that happens, the darker spirit that has been hovering over the poems all along comes into its own. "The Road at My Door" and the two poems that follow it and complete the "Meditations"—"The Stare's Nest by My Window" and "I See Phantoms of Hatred and of the Heart's Fullness and of the Coming Emptiness"—show reality crashing in on the poet's mad but engaging dream. In them he is forced to face his weakness and accept his isolation after all.

But the crucial moment of confrontation between his inner world and the destructive tidal wave of history comes in "The Road at My Door." The emotional heart of "Meditations" lies in the situation of this poem and of its central metaphor, "the cold snows of a dream." The most acutely personal poem in the twin-sequence, it also places the speaker in his impersonal historical setting, the period of the "troubles" in Ireland. The topical allusions speak for themselves.

> An affable Irregular,
> A heavily-built Falstaffian man,
> Comes cracking jokes of civil war
> As though to die by gunshot were
> The finest play under the sun.
>
> A brown Lieutenant and his men,
> Half dressed in national uniform,
> Stand at my door, and I complain
> Of the foul weather, hail and rain,
> A pear-tree broken by the storm.
>
> I count those feathered balls of soot
> The moor-hen guides upon the stream,
> To silence the envy in my thought;
> And turn towards my chamber, caught
> In the cold snows of a dream.

The "Irregulars" and the "brown" troops were rival bands of soldiers. The former belonged to the Irish Republican Army, which started the civil war against England, refusing the Dominion status agreed to by the Provisional Free State government to whose National Army the brown troops belonged. That much footnoting at least seems useful, for this is the one poem in the sequences whose emotional character is somewhat unclear if one does not know certain facts. It is important to know that the Irregular and the brown Lieutenant belong to warring factions, for that fact makes the speaker's failure to express sympathy with either one significant. The poem is full of precise detail and ambiguous feeling. *Perhaps* the speaker has a certain admiration for the highspirited Irregular although he is a happy killer—one cannot quite tell. When he complains to the Free Staters about the weather, *perhaps* he implies a worse complaint, against Ireland's miseries. And after each band in turn has left his door and returned to the outside world of murderous action and he is left alone, "caught / In the cold snows of a dream," he may be referring to more than his own unbreakable isolation and practical ineffectiveness. He may be suggesting, as well, the rigid rival idealisms of political struggle and even the opiate dream that universal peace and order prevailed in the world— the dream that had lulled the peoples before the outbreak of the Great War and all the subsequent revolutionary struggles throughout Europe.

All this is part of the poem's muted structure of ambivalences, of the way it is packed with mounting, impossible pressure. Even the affectionate phrase the speaker uses for the moor-hen's chicks that he "counts" to calm his nerves—"those feathered balls of soot"— seems to reflect that pressure. "Balls of soot" carries a penumbral suggestion of bullets and fire. And his sudden confession that he needs to "silence the envy in my thought" shows his ambivalent, near-hysterical feeling. It seems he cannot altogether repress a primitive if unworthy chagrin at not being the sort of man who "Comes cracking jokes of civil war" himself.

The politics of "The Road at My Door" is the politics of sensibility in the context of history. The poem thus embodies the whole tendency of "Meditations" and readies us for the further intensities and wider tragic scope of "Nineteen Hundred and Nineteen." Its real character lies in its movement from the robust, startled

half-ironies of the first stanza to the veiled, passive complaining of the second and finally to the chill, incon-
trovertible self-characterization of the third. The successive images spring out at us, exploding the speaker's
solitary dreaming and knocking into oblivion the noble
self-image so carefully built up in the preceding poems.
He is left, at the end, with no certainties save the unresolved anguish of his private state and the equally unresolved terror and chaos of the external world.

The next poem, "The Stare's Nest by My Window,"
provides an acerbic burning away of the ambiguities of
"The Road at My Door." Here there is no hint of admiration for swashbuckling killers, and the sequence is
locked into a position of depressive transcendence,
beyond political partisanship and firm in its private attitude. The speaker's uncertainty is now transferred from
the paralyzed inner state of the preceding poem to something more outward and empirical:

> We are closed in, and the key is turned
> On our uncertainty; somewhere
> A man is killed, or a house burned,
> Yet no clear fact to be discerned:
> Come build in the empty house of the stare.
>
> A barricade of stone or of wood;
> Some fourteen days of civil war;
> Last night they trundled down the road
> That dead young soldier in his blood:
> Come build in the empty house of the stare.
>
> We had fed the heart on fantasies,
> The heart's grown brutal from the fare;
> More substance in our enmities
> Than in our love . . .

Part of the genius of the poetic sequence as a form,
and of this pair of sequences in particular, lies in its hos-

pitality to contradictory moods and attitudes that correct or modify one another. One more instance comes in the next poem, which concludes "Meditations." Here we are back in the midst of the poet's fantasies—despite the recognition of line 11 in the passage just quoted. The title of the poem shows, however, what the two preceding poems have discovered but have not stated—how permeated dream-reverie is with "phantoms" distilled from life, projections that hardly speak of unmitigated ecstasy: "I See Phantoms of Hatred and of the Heart's Fullness and of the Coming Emptiness." The poem presents images of mob fury and counter-images of supernatural erotic female beauty, then replaces both wth a prophetic symbol of impersonal destruction—"brazen hawks" with "innumerable clanging wings that have put out the moon."

By the end of "Meditations," then, we have been taken to a place very like the arena of dark germinal consciousness in Canto 47. Out of this terror the unknown future will be born. The sequence became vibrantly painful once it touched the naked facts of Ireland's agony, in "The Road at My Door." "The Stare's Nest by My Window," equally painful, begins the shift to reconciliation that is completed, for the time being, in the final poem of "Meditations." There the dreaming mind reasserts itself, but without illusions now either about bringing practical life under meaningful control or about the poet's superiority to other men. Notice, for example, the self-mocking buffoonery of Yeats's echoing of Wordsworth's slightly solemn style in his closing sentence, and the absolute humility of this ending generally:

> I turn away and shut the door, and on the stair
> Wonder how many times I could have proved my worth
> In something that all others understand or share;

But O! ambitious heart, had such a proof drawn forth
A company of friends, a conscience set at ease,
It had but made us pine the more. The abstract joy,
The half-read wisdom of daemonic images,
Suffice the ageing man as once the growing boy.

The final note here is both humble and self-regarding,
the poet's reconciliation with his own image as the un-
heroically abstracted and introspective man he must be.
It stands in beautiful counterpoint to the music of the
preceding poem as established in its opening stanza:

The bees build in the crevices
Of loosening masonry, and there
The mother birds bring grubs and flies.
My wall is loosening; honey-bees,
Come build in the empty house of the stare.

The feeling of defeat, the feeling of possibility, are in
imperfect balance in these lines, as at the end of the closing poem. The tower's loosening masonry is a literally
observed detail but also an obvious symbol of the dis-
solving dream-structure of the earlier poems. The stares
(starlings) have built a nest there but it is empty now.
Crumbling wall and empty nest are a double image of
the speaker's condition—yet at the same time the honey-
bees are actually building in the same place. "Come
build in the empty house of the stare" is a harsh parody
of the poet's past hopes and efforts. But there is a further
implication. If there must be cyclical change, let it result
in the sweetness and fragrance of honey-bees. (Remember the "sweetness" and "gentleness" of which
founders dreamed.) These images from nature are a
quiet counter-note to the major horror and depression of
the sequence, a note picked up again in the equally subdued Wordsworthian passage at the end of the next
poem.

Still, it is a true reassertion, a persistence of open sensibility in the face of acknowledged disaster, in both passages. Again we see a process like that in Pound's poem, despite surface differences. It reveals how we "sail after knowledge" even when lost in pursuit of the dream, for the pursuit itself opens us to the grim uncertainties that make up knowledge. If this is a riddle, and a not particularly happy one, nevertheless "Nineteen Hundred and Nineteen" *leaps* into it like the swan into desolate heaven and makes a kind of triumph of confronting our blindness and inability to penetrate the universe.

The leap begins with Poem I, which as I have suggested recapitulates the emotional dynamics of "Meditations" but alters the context. The grain of feeling running through the preceding sequence persists here while the personal and local details have all but disappeared—no tower, no daydreams of founding a new élite line, no explicitly Irish allusions. It is true that there are references in Poems I, IV, and V that are clearly applicable to current events in Ireland, but they are not as tightly bound to those events as those in "Meditations." Their main function is to carry over the emotional coloration of that sequence—the sheer disappointment and sense of vileness and self-loathing—and so to help modulate the shift of key.

The new key of "Nineteen Hundred and Nineteen" is the one I have described, the leap into man's desolate existential state as the poet's major ground of awareness. The difference from "Meditations" will be clear if we compare the two opening poems. Each of them establishes the dominant emotional set of its sequence, and despite the larger scope of the former they parallel one another in form and thought. Both are in Yeats's modified ottava rima, holding him to a firm pattern which he nevertheless adapts to his idiom. The only poems in the twin-sequences to use this stanza, both are modern versions of an ancient poetic mode: the lament against mutability. Where "Ancestral Houses" laments the dead spirit of Ireland's ruling gentry, Poem I of "Nineteen Hundred and Nineteen" laments the disappearance, in time's fullness, of everything we cherish:

> Many ingenious lovely things are gone
> That seemed sheer miracle to the multitude,
> Protected from the circle of the moon
> That pitches common things about. There stood
> Amid the ornamental bronze and stone
> An ancient image made of olive wood—
> And gone are Phidias' famous ivories
> And all the golden grasshoppers and bees.

The subdued tone of this beginning, its air of dispassionate contemplation, belies its elemental sadness. The feeling makes for a special turn on the Romantic longing for the unattainable; the regret here is that, having reached perfection in certain ways, we cannot sustain it. The phrase "ingenious lovely things" rings through the poem with the memory of lost perfections and is reinforced by "sheer miracle" and, later, "famous" and "golden" and even "ornamental." Against this joyous language suggesting we are loved by smiling gods stands the word "gone" at two strategic points: the end of the first line and the beginning of the final couplet. The only active principle in the stanza is a destructive one—"the circle of the moon / That pitches common things about."

Free of any narrow local base, Poem I gathers into itself the revulsion-laden political awareness of "Meditations." Its range, though, is the whole of history, summed up in a single line: "Man is in love and loves what vanishes." The disillusionment of "Ancestral Houses" was only a prelude to the helpless, heartbroken music of this poem, whose vision is of the self-betrayal, not only of a social class, but of mankind through the ages:

> That country round
>   None dared admit, if such a thought were his,
> Incendiary or bigot could be found
> To burn that stump on the Acropolis,
> Or break in bits the famous ivories
> Or traffic in the grasshoppers or bees.

In much the same way the glimpse of "that dead young soldier in his blood" in "The Stare's Nest by My Window" is recalled but surpassed by an even more shocking image in Poem I, where it is imbedded too in language of philosophical despair over what humanity—"we"—can permit itself to be and do:

> a drunken soldiery
> Can leave the mother, murdered at her door,
> To crawl in her own blood, and go scot-free;
> The night can sweat with terror as before
> We pieced our thoughts into philosophy,
> And planned to bring the world under a rule,
> Who are but weasels fighting in a hole.

Anyone who has been shocked out of his dreams by such knowledge as this, says the poem, "has but one comfort left: all triumph would / But break upon his ghostly solitude." What was seen in the closing poems of "Meditations" as the self-indulgence of an impotent dreamer now becomes, through a conversion of spiritual energy, his one great strength. He can internalize, in the images of his art, the inhuman cyclical progression that life has forced him to confront. Poem II, for example, gives us an image of exotic dancers whose whirling

movement recalls to the speaker the ancient concept of
the "Platonic Year," a period of centuries marking vast
cycles of fated change in human life—

> It seemed that a dragon of air
> Had fallen among dancers, had whirled them round
> Or hurried them off on its own furious path;
> So the Platonic Year
> Whirls out new right and wrong,
> Whirls in the old instead . . .

But it is Poem III especially, with its swan-image and
its image of "the labyrinth" that man has made "in art or
politics," and Poem VI with its images of Herodias's
daughters returning and other, grosser archetypes that
complete the transforming conversion of defeat into a
kind of power. That conversion had a decisive sexual
dimension in Canto 47, and it is interesting that both closing poems in Yeats's double sequence introduce the
motif of the impersonal power of sexuality. At the end of
"Meditations" we see female "phantoms of the heart's
fullness" who are lost in entrancement by their own
bodily loveliness and "sweetness." At the end of "Nineteen Hundred and Nineteen" the comparable figures are
more compelling and energetic, and also vicious. In addition to Herodias' daughters with their evil "amorous
cries, or angry cries" there is the "love-lorn Lady Kyte-
ler" wooing her succubus, an "insolent fiend," with a
phallic, black-magic ritual. What seemed an image of
war-terror at the start of the poem—"Violence upon the
roads: violence of horses"—becomes by the end a symbol of vehement, mindless supernatural forces. This last
poem does precisely what Poem III says the solitary soul
must do. Its wings, "half spread for flight," are ready in
the face of these mindless phantoms of reality and imagination either "to play, or to ride / Those winds that
clamour of approaching night."

Chapter 4

Uncomfortable Choices:
ELIOT'S "LITTLE GIDDING"

Anyone reading T. S. Eliot's "Little Gidding" can readily see that his virtuosity matches Pound's and Yeats's and his method falls somewhere in between. "Little Gidding"—itself part of the famous sequence called *Four Quartets*—is divided into five qualitatively uneven segments, each self-contained enough to be a separate poem. In turn these segments have smaller units that can each be read as a separate poem. So we have a constellation of separate segments and passages in the Yeats model; and in fact, Eliot begins, as Yeats does, by revealing a scene that has stirred him to emotionally charged contemplation. But soon he moves away from the relatively static initial positioning into a less controllable orbit of association—like Pound, but always more deliberate. At high moments the process releases states of pure lyricism or dramatically crackling speech, yet the speaker holds steady within his willed frame of thought.

Eliot's genius, in large part, lies in his ability to combine the language of the most evocative immediacy with hints of deep mysteries rooted in the subtlety of his own mind. He writes in *clear* riddles. The beginning of "Little Gidding," for example, evokes the delightfully contrasty illusion of spring on a bright winter day and has a touch of the manner, say, of Hopkins's early poem "Winter with the Gulf Stream," which with gentle rapture reports the presence of summery colors and conditions in an English winter. But Eliot's lines press for something more than innocent joy at nature's sweet legerdemain. As in his most famous beginnings ("April is the cruellest month, breeding" in "The Waste Land" and "Let us go then, you and I, / When the evening is spread out against the sky / Like a patient etherised upon a table" in "The Love Song of J. Alfred Prufrock") he provides images at once simple, startling, and paradoxically suggestive of a further meaning—immanent, pressing to be revealed, yet delphic:

> Midwinter spring is its own season
> Sempiternal though sodden towards sundown,
> Suspended in time, between pole and tropic.
> When the short day is brightest, with frost and fire,
> The brief sun flames the ice, on pond and ditches,
> In windless cold that is the heart's heat,
> Reflecting in a watery mirror
> A glare that is blindness in the early afternoon.
> And glow more intense than blaze of branch, or brazier,
> Stirs the dumb spirit: no wind, but pentecostal fire
> In the dark time of the year. Between melting and freez-
>   ing
> The soul's sap quivers. There is no earth smell
> Or smell of living thing. This is the spring time
> But not in time's covenant. Now the hedgerow
> Is blanched for an hour with transitory blossom
> Of snow, a bloom more sudden
> Than that of summer, neither budding nor fading,

Not in the scheme of generation.
Where is the summer, the unimaginable
Zero summer?

The passage is more deceptive than the illusion it describes—an act of incantatory magic. Lines 4–9 and 14–16
are the only ones with concrete images from actual, ob-
servable nature. They are closer than the rest to the quality of "Winter with the Gulf Stream," which is so alive
with detail and so aroused to a melancholy-tinged gaiety
by its pure sensuous appreciation. These Hopkins-like
lines are the ones on which the imagination fastens, dazzling guides to what is meant by the impression of
"Midwinter spring." And yet they are somehow dominated by the more abstract, mystical phrasing that sur-
rounds them and that could perhaps, with some tiny
tinkering, stand by itself. Take the first three lines,
which make up the first sentence and each of which
presents a knotty proposal that mind and senses must
work together to grasp. Each presents an abstraction, yet
has its own concreteness and is in fact an image such as
an oracle might utter. The mirage of "midwinter spring"
is more than just that, is "its own season" in some revelatory religious sense. The first line, indeed, has a visionary joy that reverberates throughout the poem and
back through the earlier quartets.
    In the rest of this first sentence Eliot goes on to rein-
force and qualify the effect with acute virtuosity. The
heavy Latinism "sempiternal" at the start of the second
line modifies "season" grammatically, countering the
connotation of brevity and bolstering that of oracular
revelation like a flying buttress. It also introduces a deliberately comic note. "Sempiternal though sodden towards sundown" is a fine, ludicrous, sagging phrase for
the dimming away of illusion when the icy brilliance of

the day begins to fade. It adds an odd and dangerous tone of self-mockery, not unlike the kind we have seen in Yeats except for the compression and quick slyness of the image. "Sempiternal" dominates its line in many ways: grammatically, and by its incantatory weight, and by the clowning solemnity of its intrinsic redundancy. It even sets the alliterative norm for its line, repeating almost all the key consonants and vowels of "midwinter spring" as well. If, incidentally, we listen to the initial metrical phrases of the first three lines in relation to one another, we can hear how they control the tone of the passage. Each of them has two feet and, for the most part, plays on the same few basic sounds, and each gives an emphatically mystic thrust to its line.

What then is the affect—the specific intensity of feeling and awareness—of the whole opening stanza I have quoted? It is a double one, really, and it forces an uncomfortable choice of sensibility on both the poet and the reader. The poet needs to fuse two states of apprehension so that they are reciprocals of one another—his sensuous pleasure at the reminder of warm life and quick blossoming touched off by the sight of bright sunlight on ice or new snow on hedgerows, and his apperception of their devotional and metaphysical implications to him. He is sharply aware of the risk of forcing the issue; hence both the buffoonery and the couching of the religious implications in concrete images: "pentecostal fire," "soul's sap," "time's covenant," "heart's heat," "stirs the dumb spirit." Many, though not all of these images can be read simply as expressing the speaker's awakened excitement. Others strive to protect a tangible illusion of a state of being that exists outside time and nature, an antisensuous realm marked by the absence of "earth smell / Or smell of living thing" but alive with supernal "bloom" that is "not in the scheme of generation." The choice for the reader is one of the limits of empathy. Is the poet being tendentious and asserting the fusion by main force, or is something else going on—the presentation of an achieved, complex set of thought and feeling that has compelling elements of both sensuous and spiritual awareness and of skeptical wariness too? It is not a question of whether one agrees with Christian belief in any of its creedal forms, or with any other religious belief. Nor is it a matter of whether or not one resists, as a matter of taste or of "common sense," efforts of any kind to restore presecularist modes of thought. It is a matter, rather, of the poet's artistry in presenting a volatile condition of sensibility.

In these respects the passage is quite open to comparison with the first part of Hopkins's "The Wreck of the *Deutschland*." Hopkins convinces by the muscular effort of his language, his hard struggle to wring assent from himself to his own metaphor of crucifixion. His inconsistent, faltering ability to understand the Christian mystery is a given of the poem that he wrestles with. Eliot is subtler and stresses the illusory aspects of the sense of epiphany. He is after all more "modern" and therefore more psychologically sophisticated than he might wish to be, and he consequently mixes in some skepticism along with his desire to be devout. If he does not appeal through the music of wild struggle with himself as Hopkins does, wringing love from us by the sweat of our empathy, the language of his struggle is nevertheless there before us in all its self-contradictory paradoxicality.

When we give full attention to the first stanza of "Little Gidding," the concentrated impact of its sensibility is indeed persuasive. A sense of chill deprivation is piercingly evident. The whole atmosphere of intense cold, of the inner self's existence at zero temperature, is what gives the stanza its physical body: "frost," "ice," "wind-

less cold," "freezing," "snow," "zero." Even the imagery of brightness and light, on which the illusion of an
opposite condition depends, contributes to this atmosphere. Lines like "The brief sun flames the ice, on pond
and ditches" and "Reflecting in a watery mirror / A glare
that is blindness in the early afternoon" present shivery
winter impressions. It is true that an opposite implication is nevertheless present from the start. The implication is that this frozen inner state is precisely what gen-
erates, by laws both natural and spiritual, the imperative
need for transfiguration: "in windless cold that is the
heart's heat"—or, spelled out more decisively, "pentecostal fire / In the dark time of the year." The closing
question shows how extreme the speaker's and our deprivation is felt to be. It pursues the central oxymoron of
the first line to its exquisite ultimate terms, and with no
trace of the complacency of the assuredly saved:

> Where is the summer, the unimaginable
> Zero summer?

In the first two parts of "Little Gidding," Eliot main-
tains and develops the beautiful control and balance of
this opening movement. I am now proposing to treat
these two parts as the essential work. "Little Gidding" as
a whole is the final poem in a set of four parallel, inter-
connected pieces written over six or seven years. It has a
good deal of echoing reference to what has gone before,
and it ends with a running together of the various motifs
in the whole sequence. I have chosen to discuss it because of the great power of Parts I and II as a unit, a
power matching that of Canto 47 and the Yeats sequences. The expansive rhetoric of its later parts (as
in the case of the ending of Hopkins's "The Wreck
of the *Deutschland*") is secondary to its main force.

The immanence, the desire, the hope, the doubt sur-
rounding the suggestion of epiphany in the opening
passage establish the emotional context of the whole
curve of Parts I and II. Each of these parts has two movements, an opening passage of lyric incantation and then
a dramatic scene—a scene of expectation in the first part,
and a scene of allegorical confrontation in the second.
We have seen how the first movement opens out to us,
with an ardor and intensity undiminished by the humor
and the subtle intelligence of the passage, the possibility
of transcendent revelation in the midst of existence as we
know it. The second movement then guides us to a site
where grace is said to have been experienced in the past.
The third movement, at the beginning of Part II, is a
song about the reign of death over the material world
and the minds of those people who neglect traditional
faith. In these interim movements the sense of mystery
and awe, and of the stern discipline needed to ready
oneself for revelation, is followed by the sense of the
spirit in deadly chains if it cannot see beyond death's
secular kingdom of the four elements. In the fourth and
final movement the poem reaches its highest pitch of
power in a scene modeled on *The Divine Comedy*. Here
the speaker is simultaneously in the real and the supernatural worlds and, while not granted grace, is pointed
toward it. That is, worlds of bitter terror, from the fire-
bombing of war to the fires of hell, are set against the
glimpse of the "refining fire" of purgatory. The hints of
promised epiphany of the first movement are thus ful-
filled, but not in the terms one would have expected.

Such, in brief, is the curve of affects in Parts I and II. If
we now return to the point at which we left off earlier
on, it is interesting to see how Eliot handles the shift of
key between his first and second movements. The figure

of the "unimaginable zero summer" was a poignant
suggestion of readiness for the epiphany sensed but not
yet experienced. The question in which it was imbedded
expressed the speakers's frustration. But now, at the
beginning of the second stanza, the speaker imagines
himself as someone with authority to give a specific
reply. The quick change of role has something absurd
about it, and for an instant the speaker cannot help
clowning again and burlesquing his own presumptuous-
ness. One does not, upon asking heaven where Paradise
is to be found, expect to be handed a road map and to
hear a voice telling one just how to reach the place where
faith is rewarded by epiphany. But that is virtually what
happens here:

> Where is the summer, the unimaginable
> Zero summer?
>
>   If you came this way,
> Taking the route you would be likely to take
> From the place you would be likely to come from . . .

And so there is the one eccentric, facetious moment of
transition. It reflects the speaker's humorous awkward-
ness, counterpart of the discomfort he inflicts on the
reader by appearing to introduce a note of dogmatic certainty. The moment is soon lost as the altered voice and
tone take over. A new intelligence seems to have arrived,
descending from rapt contemplation elsewhere in specific response to the questioner. What felt like the sudden embarrassment of an actor changing roles onstage is
absorbed in its dramatic intonations. At once both se-
vere and kindly, urgent and distant, it tells us, by re-
minding us about Little Gidding, that we can all become
communicants regardless of our starting points. Little
Gidding, as all commentaries on the poem stress, is the
village where, in the seventeenth century, the devout

Anglican Nicholas Ferrar and his religious community are said to have experienced epiphany and where they were visited by Charles Stuart in his defeat.

In some ways the second movement is even subtler than the first. Its momentary buffoonery was a clue to the fact that its emotional force goes counter to its apparent doctrinal certainty. On the surface the speaking voice directs us to the site of that past moment of definite, recorded grace. Later, in the concluding stanza, it commands us to open ourselves, without inhibition by any questioning self-distancing, directly to faith:

> You are not here to verify,
> Instruct yourself, or inform curiosity
> Or carry report. You are here to kneel
> Where prayer has been valid. . . .

If this were all, the combination of travel instructions and crisp kneeling orders might simply be laughable, however touching the speaker's desire to brush doubt aside. But the whole concentration of feeling in these stanzas has to do, precisely, with our inability to guarantee spiritual certainty for ourselves no matter how fully we seek to repossess Little Gidding's visitation by the Holy Spirit. What the passage attempts is to bring into the foreground of consciousness a state of humility and faith belonging to the deep memory of England. There is no promise here, no dogma. The passage continues:

> If you came this way in may time, you would find the
>   hedges
> White again, in May, with voluptuary sweetness.
> It would be the same at the end of the journey,
> If you came at night like a broken king,
> If you came by day not knowing what you came for,
> It would be the same, when you leave the rough road
> And turn behind the pig-sty to the dull façade

> And the tombstone. And what you thought you came
>   for
> Is only a shell, a husk of meaning
> From which the purpose breaks only when it is fulfilled
> If at all. Either you had no purpose
> Or the purpose is beyond the end you figured
> And is altered in fulfilment. . . .

This is language that, as Yeats has it, longs for sweetness and gentleness—the reassurance of a sign. But what is found is a neglected, shabby scene of dreariness and death, nor is any true spiritual discovery promised as a result of the expedition. The second movement does conclude, shortly after this passage, with a richer diction that has the *sound* of spiritual transport. What is actually presented, however, is the speaker's confrontation of impenetrable mystery. Here again, as with Yeats's image of the swan leaping into desolate heaven and with Pound's Odyssean venture into the chthonic unknown, we have the predicament of heroic sensibility:

> And what the dead had no speech for, when living,
> They can tell you, being dead: the communication
> Of the dead is tongued with fire beyond the language
>   of the living.
> Here, the intersection of the timeless moment
> Is England and nowhere. Never and always.

This peroration is a bit overeloquent, given its painful concerns: the inability of the living to communicate with the dead, and the crushing oppression of being unable to get past the mind's domination by illusion. Part II meets the issue more directly, picking up from the psychological dilemma reflected in the lines just quoted. The litany on the death of all things that constitutes the poem's third movement perfectly complements the "midwinter spring" movement. Where the earlier passage clings with bright despair to the illusion of eternal presence in the midst of time, these modernized medieval stanzas descant on the vanity of all earthly concerns. A lament for the presence of mortality in each of the four elements, they begin with the very air we breathe.

> Ash on an old man's sleeve
> Is all the ash the burnt roses leave.
> Dust in the air suspended
> Marks the place where a story ended.
> Dust inbreathed was a house—
> The wall, the wainscot and the mouse.
> The death of hope and despair,
>   This is the death of air.

This is hardly cheerful, but it has a delicate lyricism that is almost buoyant. It is less heavyhearted than the second stanza, on the "death of earth," whose charnel imagery of the earth as a grave and whose high dosage of stop-sounds make it a small death-march:

> There are flood and drouth
> Over the eyes and in the mouth.

And the closing stanza, on the "death of water and fire," completes the curve of this movement by adding the burden of guilty neglect:

> Water and fire deride
> The sacrifice that we denied.
> Water and fire shall rot
> The marred foundations we forgot,
> Of sanctuary and choir. . . .

We have had, in this ever more sternly sad movement, a steel-hard recital of the pointlessness of existence without grace. Nothing in the poem so far has suggested that the spirit's journey is easy, but at least we have been shown lovely illusions and nourishing memories. But at

this death-ridden point the poem completely negates any
value dependent on mortal experience or human endeavor alone. We enter the final movement saturated
with the grimness of time, sinfulness, and death.

It is natural enough, then, that the next movement is a
Dantean passage meant to show the speaker inhabiting
his own Inferno (as so often in Eliot). It is written in a
modified terza rima to press this association. Though
dropping the traditional rhyme after the beginning, Eliot
distributes partial rhymes effectively throughout the passage and also keeps up a pattern of five-stress lines arranged in tercets. Within this fluid adaptation, his
phrasing sounds at once like Dante's and like a modern
mind's looking searingly into its own motives. Thus the
form itself dramatizes the poet's relation to the living
past of his art and to the present historical moment. The
personal crisis presented tangentially in the winter
images of Part I is seen now in his hellish encounter
with a "familiar compound ghost" on a London street
after an air raid. At the same time he is facing the coming on of old age and the "rending pain" of knowing he
can no longer mend past errors or remake himself. But
by the same token, he can recover the significant past
without being able to do anything about it. The recovery
is even more pointed now than in the visit to the restored site of Ferrar's community, for this time the past
is fiercely embodied in a human shape. The mercilessly
articulate ghost is at once the speaker's mirror-image and
a voice out of the moral and aesthetic memory of the
race—the composite voice of Dante and the other poets
who have formed the speaker's mind and art:

> I caught the sudden look of some dead master
> Whom I had known, forgotten, half recalled
> Both one and many; in the brown baked features
> The eyes of a familiar compound ghost

Both intimate and unidentifiable.
    So I assumed a double part, and cried
    And heard another's voice cry: "What! are *you* here?"
Although we were not. I was still the same,
    Knowing myself yet being someone other—
    And he a face still forming . . .

The atmosphere, so powerfully Dantean, recalls various recognition scenes in the *Inferno* and in *Purgatory*, particularly those with Brunetto Latini and Arnaut Daniel. It also recalls Odysseus's meeting with Tiresias in Book XI of the *Odyssey* and the way Pound, in Canto 1, picks up Tiresias's outcry at seeing Odysseus amid the shades summoned up from Erebus. These are all significant meetings under conditions of horror. Some, especially in Dante, are full of affection and sympathy despite the circumstances. Eliot extends the feeling to imply a strange, ambiguously reciprocal identity of speaker and ghost, so that the latter is both a psychological projection of the speaker and a separate apparition. The phrasing as a whole suggests that the speaker, racked by the most vulnerable responsiveness, is a double personality in process of formation. Under the impact of the articulate past his sense of himself becomes eerily complex, as with Pound in Canto 47.

The movement of the Dantean episode occurs during a relatively short interval of time, long enough for poet and ghost to meet under seemingly hurried conditions and to exchange greetings as they tread the pavement "in a dead patrol," for the poet to entreat an oracular message, and for the ghost to make a thirty-six-line reply and disappear. Beginning "In the uncertain hour before the morning" and ending as day breaks, the whole seventy-two-line episode takes place between the disappearance of the last Nazi bombing-plane of the night and the first sight of damaged streets in the morning:

> In the uncertain hour before the morning
>   Near the ending of interminable night
>   At the recurrent end of the unending
> After the dark dove with the flickering tongue
>   Had passed below the horizon of his homing
>   While the dead leaves till rattled on like tin
> Over the asphalt where no other sound was
>   Between three districts whence the smoke arose
>   I met one walking, loitering and hurried

and:

> The day was breaking. In the disfigured street
>   He left me, with a kind of valediction,
>   And faded on the blowing of the horn.

Between these opening and closing passages the episode moves through a variety of demanding affects. The opening lines reflect the combined monotony, anxiety, and mounting tension of an air raid by their word-play on the idea of its ever ending: "near the ending," "interminable," "recurrent end," and "unending." And then the plane itself is a deadly parody of the dove of annunciation, a perverse manifestation of the supernatural. The images of dead leaves and of smoke rising where the bombs have fallen suggest spectres in a fiery urban hell. And there is the sudden appearance of the ghost, who provides the point of focus for the rest of the movement.

The ghost's long speech has its own dynamics. In itself it presents a sudden jump from the traumatized atmosphere of blitzed London that has shocked the poet into utter receptivity and need for instruction. The situation is comparable to that in "The Road at My Door," both because of the violent context and because of the poet's discovery of his dream-bound solitude. "I may not comprehend, may not remember," he says to the ghost, who as I have suggested is in large part a projection of his own deepest self. When the ghost does speak, it is not of war but of the poet's embittered and damned state as man and artist. Certain phrases in the third movement—"ash on an old man's sleeve," "the death of hope and despair," "the vanity of toil" "laughs without mirth," and "the sacrifice that we denied"—now take on a harsh personal meaning that makes the litany seem less a ritually stylized (though beautifully developed) set piece than it did at first.

Brusquely the ghost cuts into the poet's self-regard, accusing him of a kind of betrayal: "My thoughts and theory which you have forgotten." The reference, though ambiguous, seems to be the poet's abandonment of his own driving principles. If it shows remorse over his growth as an artist, the feeling must have to do with a disparity between a Dantean task he once envisioned for himself, in which utmost power of moral imagination would inform extreme discipline of technique, and a present sense that he has botched the task. (Another phrase from the litany, "the marred foundations we forgot," makes itself felt here.) The ghost's dry disgust in describing the vanity of all artistic toil suggests the poet's deep fear of becoming obsolete:

> "Last season's fruit is eaten
> And the fullfed beast shall kick the empty pail.
> For last year's words belong to last year's language
> And next year's words await another voice."

Remembering the enormous yearning at the start of the poem for the timeless and supernatural to manifest itself, presumably so that the soul can find itself in the bright sunlight of eternal joy, one can only feel that as epiphanies go this is a rather disappointing one. The encounter with the ghost both fulfils and redirects the high expectations of the poem. We are not in Paradise but in a

no man's land between the world of death and the world
of spiritual suffering beyond death. Earthly and un-
earthly hell and purgatory have become indistinguishable, and so there is easy commerce between them.
As the ghost puts it:

> "But, as the passage now presents no hindrance
>   To the spirit unappeased and peregrine
>   Between two worlds become much like each other,
> So I find words I never thought to speak"

Another dimension of the poet's fear of being obsolete,
incidentally, is the suggestion that poetry itself is obsolete in our time. If so, there would indeed have been
"vanity of toil." The ghost, the far side of the speaker's
isolated self, speaks of the poet's cleansing and prophetic
role in the past tense only:

> Since our concern was speech, and speech impelled us
>   To purify the dialect of the tribe
>   And urge the mind to aftersight and foresight . . .

But the ghost, if not the living poet in his own right,
embodies the past meanings of the art at the point where
they impinge on the present. He, rising gloomily out of
all previous history, can still speak directly in the old
prophetic spirit. When he does so, it is to disclose to the
poet "the gifts reserved for age" that will "set a crown
upon your lifetime's effort." It is a new litany of loss,
stinging in its personal bearing: "the cold friction of ex-
piring sense," "the conscious impotence of rage," and
"the rending pain of re-enactment" of a lifetime's irreversible errors and harmful acts. Then, against all this
crush of fatality and regret, the ghost's concluding sentence—in the penultimate tercet of the passage—sings
out in a new key:

"From wrong to wrong the exasperated spirit
   Proceeds, unless restored by that refining fire
   Where you must move in measure, like a dancer."

The brilliant simplicity of the Dantean encounter is beautifully concentrated in this one transforming moment. Up to this point it had seemed that whole tragic framework might be reduced to a complaint about old age and the loss of status of the poet's métier. A line like the one just preceding this tercet—"Then fools' approval stings, and honour stains"—has a fine Popean ring, but the tercet has full prophetic authority. We are still in the depths, but the voice now reminds us that the realm of vision is not unremittingly infernal. Grace is even here not promised, but it is a possibility that one can still imagine waiting beyond the purgatorial suffering of the present. That suffering *can* be felt, in Dante's phrase, as a "refining fire." The modifying clause "Where you must move in measure, like a dancer" implies an inspiriting value after all in the processes of art. The condition of this vision is still that of the "midwinter spring" movement, all desire and potentiality, though the context now is fire rather than ice. But it is the process of poetic dialectic, "in measure, like a dancer," that has brought us to this new stage of realization.

The buoyancy of this reoriented vision is all the more remarkable when one considers that the refining fire is a form of torment. The elation of a glimmer of hope is the major feeling, however. It is supported in the closing tercet that follows by the image of daybreak and by the phrases "a kind of valediction" and "the blowing of the horn." At the very end, we are back on the "disfigured street" of the bombed city, as desolate as before and yet liberated from the utterly charnel atmosphere at the start

of the episode. The city's smoking rubble and the purgatorial image of "refining fire" have been irrevocably
linked.

Had Ezra Pound been shown "Little Gidding" in
manuscript as some two decades earlier he had been
shown "The Waste Land," he might well have advised
Eliot to be content with just the first two parts—however
disastrous for the mechanical symmetry of *Four Quartets*.
Although mitigated by wonderful lines and by the flick-
ering presence of Eliot's unique sensibility, the heavy
dose of sheer prosiness constitutes a real barrier in the
rest of the poem. One can see the kind of change that
takes place if one looks again at the end of Part II and
then at the opening of Part III:

> "From wrong to wrong the exasperated spirit
>   Proceeds, unless restored by that refining fire
>   Where you must move in measure, like a dancer."
> The day was breaking. In the disfigured street
>   He left me, with a kind of valediction,
>   And faded on the blowing of the horn.
>
>   III
> There are three conditions which often look alike
> Yet differ completely, flourish in the same hedgerow:
> Attachment to self and to things and to persons, detach-
>   ment
> From self and from things and from persons; and, growing
>   between them, indifference
> Which resembles the others as death resembles life . . .

Eliot is here explaining what he has already implied daz-
zlingly. It is like explaining the roses in the Muse's hair,
or the fragrance of her breasts. But I do not wish to labor
this point. My intention is not to denigrate the rest of
"Little Gidding" but to isolate the essential poem within
it.

I shall have more to say about *Four Quartets* in a later

chapter, for it is a sequence of great interest. One more word may be in order here, however. The most exquisitely made of the *Quartets* is "Burnt Norton," the only one written before the war. It was this poem that set the pattern (and hence, to some degree, set the trap) for the rest. Its lyrical control is more consistent than that of "Little Gidding." Where its rhythm goes intentionally slack, the poem is marred but moves quickly on to regain its momentum—as "Little Gidding" cannot do because it becomes overloaded with such writing. In "Burnt Norton" the opening movement evokes the illusion of epiphany almost as poignantly as does the "midwinter spring" movement, and it too has an *Inferno*-like passage that is grim enough though not as passionate and dynamic as the encounter later on. In many ways it is an improvisation of unparalleled skill, with enough carryover to provide a basis for the poems that follow it. The *Quartets* return again and again to the same preoccupations. All seek the manifestation of the eternal at a point, the yearning mind of the poet, where the memory of the past intersects with the experience of the present and with the immanent future. On this search the speaker brings to bear his recollections of special moments when desire and frustration and taunting illusion chimed together like a music of loss and promise. A constant factor, too, is the recurrent emergence of the poet in his own right, complaining in certain passages about the impossibility of making something permanent out of the perishable materials of his art.

Under the special pressure of the war and the London blitz, Eliot discovered latent energies that enabled him to recapture, in "Little Gidding," the ultimate emotional force his work had lacked for a number of years. Be that as it may, the Dantean episode burst the chains of his self-echoing patterns in the *Quartets* and, in sheer

power, surpasses their best previous achievement. And
that previous achievement is manysided. There are, for
instance, those passages I have mentioned that show the
poet's exasperated struggle to make language hold still:

> Words strain,
> Crack and sometimes break, under the burden,
> Under the tension, slip, slide, perish,
> Decay with imprecision, will not stay in place . . .
>
> ("Burnt Norton")

And there are high imagist moments throughout the
poems. One cannot do better than achieve the stirring
accuracy and resonances of images or image-clusters
such as these. One instance among the many:

> The salt is on the briar rose,
> The fog is in the fir trees.
> The sea howl
> And the sea yelp, are different voices
> Often together heard: the whine in the rigging,
> The menace and caress of wave that breaks on water,
> The distant rote in the granite teeth,
> And the wailing warning from the approaching headland
> Are all sea voices, and the heaving groaner
> Rounded homewards, and the seagull . . .
>
> ("The Dry Salvages")

Such incomparable effects of tone and impression
make up the real organic body of *Four Quartets*. Yet
while they contribute so much, the Dantean episode
goes beyond them in its full tragic impact. Through it
the iron enters the soul of "Little Gidding," and as a
result the failure of the planned architectural scheme to
work completely hardly matters. Also, the fact that there
are effective patches of poetry within the three heavily
didactic final parts helps to redeem them in the wake of
that great climax. Thus, the second movement of Part III

begins with a touching affirmation, in a medieval idiom that rings out like the most melodious of bells:

> Sin is Behovely, but
> All shall be well, and
> All manner of thing shall be well.

And there are moments that quietly echo the Dantean notes of tragedy and distant promise.

> If I think of a king at nightfall,
> Of three men, and more, on the scaffold
> And a few who died forgotten
> In other places, here and abroad,
> And of one who died blind and quiet . . .

The uncomfortable choice pressed on us by Eliot's tendentiousness is still a factor. But where a work has the poetic strengths of the first two parts of "Little Gidding," the essential poem makes itself felt even if a fair part of the work is relatively inoperative. Eliot himself felt that the didactic Christian message should not be left to mere inference. His emotional center in the poem is uncertain, still fixed in the subtle ambiguities of memory and sensuous awareness it was his special genius to command and yet, more and more, ready to attach itself to the rhetorical and meditative values of religious discourse. It is therefore hardly strange that he could soar to a height from which he dominated the whole sequence with one blazing, decisive moral vision before he climbed down again, explaining his ideas happily all during the descent. Eliot was closer to their method than the new theoreticians of poetic process have realized. He too took the risk of bringing the whole baggage of his mind along, cluttering the aesthetic field of action as he went. I have suggested that the formal pattern he devised to put the *Quartets* in harmony with one another and to create a genuine progression at the same time helped him to bring the passionate vision of the Dantean episode into the structure as its great climactic moment, the embodiment of everything fed into it over the years. On the other hand, it prevented his recasting the work so that the inner poem in process could find its most effective form. But there we are, at just the heart of the poetic issue—the fact that all structure is tentative and a matter of energies that may or may not be susceptible to remobilization and reorientation.

PART II

*ESSENTIAL
POETIC PRESENCE*

Chapter 5

Dimensions of Pound:
THE STRUCTURING OF *THE CANTOS*

Here is a poem from Pound's *Ripostes* (1912), published when he was twenty-seven.

IN EXITUM CUIUSDAM
On a certain one's departure

"Time's bitter flood"! Oh, that's all very well,
But where's the old friend hasn't fallen off,
Or slacked his hand-grip when you first gripped fame?
I know your circle and can fairly tell
What you have kept and what you've left behind:
I know my circle and know very well
How many faces I'd have out of mind.

The poem is a relatively unknown model of what might be called Pound's innate virtuosity. The phrasing is colloquially toughminded, even cynical, and yet is lyrically mobilized as well. In form the poem is an original improvisation. It begins with a line that thrusts two entirely different tones at us, in a roughened variation from the iambic pentameter that will prevail; and it withholds its rhymes until the second half. No clear pattern, then, controls the initial effect of spontaneity. When the rhymes do emerge, the key one—the repeated "very well"—is an identical rhyme. Two other repetitions, of "grip" and "circle," both of them stressing hard insights into the social and literary pecking orders, help make up the inner design. So, of course, does the alliterative pattern, especially of *f*'s, which give a crisp emphasis to the bitter or cynical phrases in which they occur.

One notes, in addition, indications (tiny buds, that is) of the methods Pound would use a few years later in *The Cantos*. There is for instance the Latin title, kindly translated in the subtitle. And as with Canto 47, the poem erupts with an isolated exclamation in relation to which the succeeding lines arrange themselves. The exclamation is never explained. In context it can be understood only as a rueful outcry by the "certain one" of the title, presumably now famous, at the passage of time—an outcry meant to explain his losing touch with former friends. The rest of the poem is then a caustically worldly reply, together with an equally caustic self-characterization. The whole piece has a Flaubertian sophistication and rigor of style.

The phrase "time's bitter flood" originally appeared in another very short poem, Yeats's "The Lover Pleads with His Friends for Old Friends," which was written some fifteen years earlier. Once we read this poem we can see how Pound has used it and yet made virtually everything in it his own.

> Though you are in your shining days,
> Voices among the crowd
> And new friends busy with your praise,
> Be not unkind or proud,
> But think about old friends the most:

> Time's bitter flood will rise,
> Your beauty perish and be lost
> For all eyes but these eyes.

Yeats's love poem reaches its climax in the final three lines, beginning "Time's bitter flood will rise." It makes a subtle and personal turn on two traditional themes, the mutability lament and the *carpe diem* admonition, and the second and third lines introduce a suggestion, just the barest, of social pressure and competition. The note of romantic glamor set up by the lovely phrase "your shining days" is somewhat sustained by "unkind" and "proud" and the slightly archaic "Be not" of the fourth line and then expanded into the swelling music of the ending. Pound picks up the key phrase in that music, and the word "friend" (a deliberate understatement in Yeats), and the essential structure in which the ending is like an arrow released by the plea that precedes it. In Pound's poem the opening exclamation is the delphic center, like the first line of Canto 47: "Who even dead, yet hath his mind entire!" Both beginnings transform memorable quotations into such centers by adding exclamation points that isolate them as mysterious shouts in the mind's still depths. The shouted quotation from Yeats—"Time's bitter flood"!—floats there at the start, holding firm against everything the speaker has to say. The confidential, sardonic sentence that follows it floats alongside, in an entirely different voice. Then comes the assertive confession at the end, which suddenly makes the poem much more than a knowing gibe at Yeats's phrase. These two lines bring the merely incidental world of "the crowd" and of "new friends," a world scorned and feared in Yeats's poem, emphatically into Pound's poem. They complete the little sensibility-mobile, made up of three sets of awareness.

"In Exitum Cuiusdam" is hardly as accomplished as a number of Pound's other poems written at about the same time. One might note, for instance, three poems that reveal his special talent for conjuring up the mentality of eras and cultures far different from our own. These are his translation of the Anglo-Saxon poem "The Seafarer," his rhapsodic incantation "The Alchemist," and his visionary poem "The Return," of which Yeats generously said that it expressed the spirit of his book *A Vision* better than any poem of his own. But "In Exitum Cuiusdam" adds the dimension of the acutely evoked present. It is not necessarily directed at Yeats himself, yet is an intimate rejoinder cheekily calculated to remind any romantic protestant against the way of the world of a thing or two. (Pound does tease Yeats, a friend twenty years his senior, now and then in his poems—for example in the pleasant parody called "The Lake Isle.") The poem is an early instance of Pound's sense of his own presence in the society of the real poets, among men and women who are introspective and self-conscious yet outspoken too. Also, the poem's response to Yeats's metaphor for time and change reveals a constant reality of Pound's mind: its absorption in phrases that resonate through the imagination. Pound brings his private and his professional selves into much of his poetry, along with the world of past and present as he knows it.

A more expanded instance, "Villanelle: the Psychological Hour," appeared in *Lustra* (1915). Here Pound, echoing a tonal gesture of Eliot's, *almost* presents himself as a kind of Prufrock. He knew Eliot's poem well, of course, having arranged for its publication in *Poetry* magazine. "The Love Song of J. Alfred Prufrock" had actually been written in 1910–11, long before "Villanelle" was composed. The sensibilities of both young poets had so much in common, despite their great differences

of energy and some important differences of point of
view, that we are dealing with something other than
simple imitation. But the very beginning of Pound's
poem is certainly reminiscent of "Prufrock"—

> I had over-prepared the event,
>   that much was ominous.
> With middle-ageing care
>   I had laid out just the right books.

A bit further on we come to the line " 'Their little
cosmos is shaken,' " which makes one think of Eliot's
"Do I dare disturb the universe?" And in general the
speakers in both poems share a certain embarrassment at
their own frustrated attempts to establish a much desired
intimacy. They engage in self-mockery; their monologues have certain comparable images. Eliot's "lonely
men in shirt-sleeves, leaning out of windows" are clearly
matched, for instance, by Pound's "And now I watch,
from the window, / the rain, the wandering busses." It
was not that Pound could not think of his own images,
or write in a tone unlike Eliot's. But in this poem he
builds a music and a structure of his own out of communion with and reaction to the Prufrock-intonation, just as
he did with the Homeric note at the start of Canto 47 and
the Yeatsian one in "In Exitum Cuiusdam."

What the poems share primarily is an atmosphere of
self-conscious loneliness so nakedly displayed it is almost shameful. But as "Villanelle" progresses we see
that its resemblances to "Prufrock" come mostly at the
start. Stylistic differences appear, and the dramatic situation is more sharply focused in Pound's poem. First of all
(last of all in the poem's own movement), we are told
that the protagonist is Pound himself, presented as a
poet who is going through a period of crisis. The literal
details given are that he is eager to develop a friendship

with two people—presumably a young couple—who promise to call on him but never do. Why all this means so much to him is never revealed, but it is certainly related to his special need in this period for intimate contacts. The parallel to Prufrock's condition does not disappear entirely, but the *poem*'s character changes by the end. The brief third section that concludes the poem breaks away from introspection entirely:

> Now the third day is here—
>   no word from either;
> No word from her nor him,
> Only another man's note:
>   "Dear Pound, I am leaving England."

The abruptness of this ending marks a considerable shift from the two preceding sections. The long opening movement is in part mood-setting anecdote, in part meditation, and in part song. The second section is an anxious internal dialogue in which the poet reconstructs his recent evening in the company of the couple and various literati and tries to gauge the impression he made on them. The final movement, just quoted, is sharply objective although it irreversibly slams down the lid on the poet's hopes. If the poem is a subtle, hypersensitive picture of a devastating "psychological hour," it is also a painfully focused glimpse of an elusive side of social life that includes the charming mirages sometimes flashed before us. There is a wry and worldly intelligence here alongside the vulnerable sensibility, the same kind of intelligence that, in "In Exitum Cuiusdam," picked up and responded warily to Yeats's rich diction: " 'Time's bitter flood!' Oh, that's very well." In "Villanelle" too we find a deflating expression—almost the same words: "Oh, I know well enough"—

"Their little cosmos is shaken"—
        the air is alive with that fact.
In their parts of the city
        they are played on by diverse forces.
How do I know?
        Oh, I know well enough.
For them there is something afoot.
        As for me:
I had over-prepared the event—

      Beauty is so rare a thing
      So few drink of my fountain.

Two friends: a breath of the forest . . .
Friends? Are people less friends
    because one has just, at last, found them?
Twice they promised to come.

     "Between the night and morning?"

Beauty would drink of my mind.
Youth would awhile forget
        my youth is gone from me.

I quote this passage at length because it catches the music of the mind in the act of talking things over with itself, and because the italicized lines impose an overlay of song on that music of related feeling. Serious in the main but self-mocking at the same time, the poem gains an impersonal beauty from these italicized lines—at first both plaintive and precarious in their near-preciosity, then suggestive of time-disorientation and passion, and finally both abstract and bemused. They emphasize the melodic arrangement of the rest of the poem, particularly the counterpointing of line-segments indicated by typographical breaks.

The transfer of musical energy thus produced is especially useful in the two lines that close the passage. These lines hint faintly at a greater loss than the momentary letdown of an undeveloped friendship: "Youth would awhile forget / my youth is gone from me." The desire here is for a life of "forgetting" not really open to a person like the speaker. The level of his awareness has hardly allowed him to have a heedless youth. The world of unexamined experience is that of "the forest" from which the pair who did not come might have brought along "a breath." So long as he does not really know them he may imagine them thus, as inhabitants of Arden. Had they come, they would have been like wild creatures seeking to drink of his fountain: *"Beauty would drink of my mind."* And there is the trick his imagination plays on him. For it would still be to him as a poet, or as a Platonic guardian of beauty, that the two would have come, rather than simply giving themselves to joys of youthful friendship. (And perhaps, since he does speak of "my fountain" and "my mind," that is what he would really wish after all.) So the speaker is still, like Yeats, lost in the cold snows of a dream—of affectionate companionship, of escaping the isolation of his awareness. This desolation with which he is left at the end of the first movement carries over to the even bleaker feeling of the concluding movement, already quoted. There the sense of the void is confirmed by the curt farewell-note he receives—an abandonment by yet a third person. The final movement is full of negatives: "no word from either / No word from her nor him." Even the words "now" and "note" in the five-line ending take on negative coloration because they echo the sounds of "no" and "nor."

Assimilation of life's plenitude into his created world is Pound's artistic program. Sometimes he succeeds gloriously, and sometimes he is alienated from the intractable world of things as they are. Hence the curious and compelling balance of energies in Pound's writing as he wrestles with this central concern of art and idealism.

We see the balance on a tiny scale in the contrasts of "In Exitum Cuiusdam," and on a more complex, though still limited, one in "Villanelle: the Psychological Hour." Success is a matter of the intensity with which the assimilation is projected in a structure that may well involve many points of attention in a single curve of aroused discovery. Pound's urge to do a very long poem in interlinked segments grows out of his need to follow this program to its limits.

I have, obviously, been leading up to *The Cantos*. Before I turn to them, I want to offer just a few observations on *Hugh Selwyn Mauberley (Life and Contacts)*, published in 1920. The parenthetical subtitle indicates that this sequence of eighteen poems (divided into a 1919 group of thirteen poems and a 1920 group of five poems) has the aim I have been discussing. It is a double sequence, in which the first part systematically criticizes modern European life and culture—especially the British manifestations—from the viewpoint of a disenchanted young American poet with an exalted sense of artistic traditions. His mind alive with the language of poetic masterpieces since Homer, he has been seeking to locate and rekindle the right sources for a vital modern poetry in English. The first part of the sequence is angry and sardonic and displays a dazzling lyrical range. The second part, "Mauberley (1920)," retraces the ground of the first in subjective, self-reductive language that reflects the poet's fear of being unable to perform his high artistic mission. Since Pound had already begun *The Cantos* when he wrote *Mauberley*, we may well note some aspects of the shorter sequence that make it a simpler model toward the construction of *The Cantos*.

Mauberley is a complete work of great interest in itself, but at the same time it served as testing-ground for working with a float of alternative selves or personae. If

the title has any relevance, it indicates that the protagonist of the poem is named Hugh Selwyn Mauberley. Yet
Mauberley is not named in the text of any of the poems
and the title of very first poem is "E. P. Ode pour l'Elec-
tion de son Sepulchre." That title brings Pound himself
into the poems from the start. Moreover, many of the details about the protagonist—his nationality, his preoccupations, and even his identification with Odysseus in
that same first poem—are autobiographical and call the
fact to our attention. Like Pound, he has been living in
England because of the lure of a siren-song: the hope of
reviving the classical spirit there by helping create a
modern poetry that will have the precision, elegance,
and sinew of the best writing of modern France: "His
true Penelope was Flaubert."

The deliberate ambiguity of the protagonist, this Mau-
berley-Pound-Odysseus, enables the poet to work with
many degrees of intensity and varieties of feeling and
style in creating the reciprocities of this sequence. It is
interesting that, while most of the poems are in the first
person, the ones that are most intimately self-analytical
and personal in their reference are distanced by being
put in the third person. Despite its heavy infusion of
irony and literary allusion, the first poem is one of
these—a mock elegy for himself because his doom as a
poet has been pronounced by establishment authorities.
The second and third poems, and to some degree the
fourth, in the second section are deeply introspective
and confess the fear of significant weaknesses in the protagonist's character and work. I do not wish to linger
over *Mauberley* here, but its mixture of tones and perspectives and its dynamics of movement from one poem
to the next, as well as its deployment of so wide a range
of pointed literary echoes and allusions, ally it in many
ways to *The Cantos*.

It is the structure of *The Cantos,* which have played a major role in making us aware of the modern sequence as a genre, to which I want to turn attention now. It needs no oracle to tell us that they are an extreme example of the form. They are, in fact, a sequence of sequences, each growing out of the interests and experiences of a limited period of time. It would be ludicrous for us to imagine that the whole line of succeeding sets of cantos, developing for almost fifty years, constitutes a single integrated work in any ordinary sense. The normal process of getting a work under way, discovering its proper form and bearings, and revising it so that the whole can emerge as organically as possible is simply not open to a poet who writes out of the successive phases of his life, in chronological order, without leaving time for recasting.

Pound could not possibly, for example, have known in advance that he was going to write *The Pisan Cantos,* based on his period as a prisoner in an American detention camp in Italy after World War II. Nor, once *A Draft of XVI Cantos* appeared in 1925, did he ever again take the opportunity to reconceive, reconstruct, and reorient the whole of what he had so far written. (One delayed influence of *The Cantos,* by the way, has been the spate in recent years of sequences "arranged" on a purely chronological basis, often self-destructing as they sputter along.) The individual groupings of cantos are another matter. They correspond to the succeeding volumes of poetry of any prolific writer, with the usual repetitions of motif and of the deeper emotional and character-revealing strains, as well as of certain idioms of form. The need to assert a heroic program for controlling the long-range destiny of his art was perhaps a trap laid by Pound's psyche in his early middle age, similar to the one Eliot was to lay for himself in *Four Quartets.* It was also a compulsion, however, and so there is an *insistent* continuity whether or not there is an organic one.

Nevertheless, even after one grants this last point, it still seems best to view each new group of cantos, not as an integral part of a single unfolding work but as a re-casting, or redirecting with new elements added: start-ing all over again each time, as it were. This, after all, is the process whenever any poet brings out a new collec-tion. But because Pound repeats effects again and again, and endlessly creates momentary tensions and balances of a recognizable sort—for instance, his device of suddenly coming out of a welter of notations and allu-sions with an effect of pure song or vision—he gains a certain complex consistency of texture. Moment by mo-ment in many cantos we have a sort of Brownian move-ment, a process of bombardment of the speaking sensi-bility by disparate impressions, associations, and emotional sparks. The sensibility seems endlessly fluid and receptive. Something of the same sort happens in Browning. (The pun, though unconscious, is hardly ac-cidental.) With him too we often move through a chaos of sensation and thought, barely manageable, toward ex-alted or depressed encompassments, and suddenly things hold firm for an unexpected instant of epiphany. Or the reverse happens. The process is more drastic in Pound, though. It reveals itself swiftly, at the end of Canto 1. Here the intensely repossessed, ultimately tragic epic moment breaks—brilliantly—under the pres-sure of its own released associations, locked till now in the speaker's mind. From here on, it will always be a question where the ascendancy lies: whether in the con-trolling imagination; or in the irrepressible and torment-ing associative energies of the speaker, his head full of ineradicable voices and faces and pictures; or in the serendipity that generally attends a skilled artist, regardless of how the images and thoughts that assail him have arrived.

Pound's careful reworking of the first cantos has been described by Miles Slatin and others.* Looking at the structure of *A Draft of XVI Cantos* in its final form, we can see a clear progression of tones emerging from within the fluid context. The Odyssean overture plunges us into the midst of deeply serious action—that is, *poetic* action. We are in an awe-filled ancient world, with the hero who has lain with the goddess and has now been bidden to seek out the terrifying realm of the dead. The first movement of the canto is largely tragic, with the "impetuous impotent dead" crowding about Odysseus and the pathetic account of Elpenor and the harsh practicality of the hero's meeting his own mother and beating her off, and then the grim words of Tiresias. *The Cantos,* then, begin with the language of dread and daring of the *Nekuia* (Book XI of the *Odyssey*). The language seems even more archaically powerful and simple because of Pound's concentrated translation, strongly influenced by the sixteenth-century Latin translation of Andreas Divus.

But this elementary affect is given a kaleidoscopic whirl when we find that the speaker is not actually Odysseus but a modern sensibility ("Pound," if that were not too simplified a way of putting it) returning as Odysseus *redivivus*—"a second time," although that event never occurred in the *Odyssey*. Pound seems to have got the idea for this marvelous turn from Divus's *iterum*,† most likely intended as an intensive. In sud-

---

*See Miles Slatin, "A History of Pound's Cantos I–XVI, 1915–1925," *American Literature* 35 (1963), 183–95.
†See Ezra Pound, *Literary Essays* (Norfolk, Conn.: New Directions, 1954), p. 262:

> "Cur iterum o infelix linquens lumen Solis
> Venisti, ut videas mortuos, et iniucundum regionem?"

denly altered perspective, the whole play of language
enters a Picasso-world of multiple dimensions. The
Anglo-Saxon kennings and alliteration, the free verse adaptation of rhythmic pattern to suggest ancient ritual and
incantation, are not merely translation technique, admirable as that would be in itself. They also project a sophisticated modern mind, aware of varied cultural traditions and literary usages as *resources:* Divus as a bridge
to Homer, kennings as hard images in the modern sense
that yet evoke the formulaic ritual of Homeric and Old
English poetry, Odysseus as an avatar of the awe and
strangeness, the *terror,* we must feel when we undertake
to explore the deepest mysteries of existence. We have
been all but invisibly prepared for that breaking forth of
the modern voice toward the end of the canto—"Lie
quiet Divus"—and for the riddling images in praise of
Aphrodite that follow, still echoing Homer but releasing
the natural voice of a witty, image-savoring, culture-
comparing intelligence.

And Anticlea came, whom I beat off, and then Tiresias The-
     ban,
Holding his golden wand, knew me, and spoke first:
"A second time? why? man of ill star,
Facing the sunless dead and this joyless region?
Stand from the fosse, leave me my bloody bever
For soothsay."
            And I stepped back,
And he strong with the blood, said then: "Odysseus
Shalt return through spiteful Neptune, over dark seas,
Lose all companions." And then Anticlea came.
Lie quiet Divus. I mean, that is Andreas Divus,
In officina Wecheli, 1538, out of Homer.
And he sailed, by Sirens and thence outward and away
And unto Circe.
            Venerandam,
In the Cretan's phrase, with the golden crown, Aphrodite,

Cypri munimenta sortita est, mirthful, orichalchi, with golden
Girdles and breast bands, thou with dark eyelids
Bearing the golden bough of Argicida. So that:

Until this final stanza, the seriousness has been unbroken. The poem has been a straightforward repossession
of the world of Homer's Book XI—straightforward, that
is, in purpose; the sheer technique devoted to catching
the living original quality of the text required a most
subtle ear. The first ten lines of this stanza are equally
serious and straightforward: altogether locked into the
deeply archaic *Nekuia*. A modern voice now enters the
poem, serious in its own way and yet making a joke. It
tells Divus to stop turning in his grave, for Pound is giving his translation full credit and even naming Wechel's
Paris workshop where Divus's book was printed. For the
moment, Homer's world of mythic awe is dispersed by
the flip command. The qualities of Odysseus nevertheless remain models for this intruding modern poetic intelligence, which would already use the hero as a touchstone in the fashion we have observed in Canto 47. The
speaker is pulling together whatever visionary insight he
can muster from all he has read and imagined—for instance, from Homeric Hymn II, addressed to Aphrodite,
which was translated into Latin by Georgius Dartona
Cretensis ("the Cretan"). There Aphrodite, goddess of
sexual beauty and therefore of earth's treasures (gold and
orichalchi—copper) is praised as Cyprus's protectress.
Pound links her with fertility rites ("the golden bough")
and, as "Argicida" (Greek-slayer), with war.

"Cretensis" described Aphrodite as "venerandam"—
to be worshiped. She embodies the female sexual principle that is an equivalent to fate in Canto 47. Here, however, she is introduced into the poem in the midst of its
sudden tonal shift from the archaic, fiercely compelling

archetypes of the *Odyssey* to the volatile, open perspectives of our century. It is important to recognize the simple dynamics of feeling in the poem's rapidly refocused final stanza. First we have the increasing tempo of the sense of tragic strangeness; then, the shock of readjustment when Tiresias asks, "A second time?"—and then the rich little passage of praise for the female-erotic, Aphrodisian principle. The mythic, heroic, tragic evocations have been realized into by an aroused, definitely modern mind, which brings them to bear in a new, sexual, but still myth-saturated context. The canto casts a long shadow: not only over cantos written many years later linking the Odyssean with the chthonian and the erotic, but over the rest of *A Draft of XVI Cantos*. The visit of Odysseus *redivivus* to the world of the dead serves as a context for the cartoon-like hell-cantos, the fourteenth and fifteenth. It also prepares us for the Dantean scene that opens Canto 16 and for the plunge thereafter into the modern hell of World War I. That was the curve of movement of Pound's first book of cantos: from the evocation of the world of Homer's Book of the Dead to the symbolic hell of modern capitalism to the scene, as in Dante, of moral torment at the start of Canto 16 and the climactic panorama of war and violence and corruption at the end. The tonal links are between the tragic awe of Odysseus before the dead and that of Blake before Hell-mouth, and between the jeering disgust of the hell-cantos and the atmosphere of loss and waste at the end of Canto 16.

The erotic note introduced in Canto 1 is picked up in Canto 2, where it acquires new dimensions. The Aphrodite passage has a strategic location at the end of Canto 1. Also, its style, so different from that of the preceding lines, gives it strong emphasis. So does its suspension in mid-air, which suggests a grammatical link to the next canto. Nevertheless, it remains a subordinate if striking section of its canto. The Odysseus passage holds priority in its elemental grandeur of death-obsession and obsession with irreversible fatality, while the canto's ending only introduces the counterthrust of life-affirmation in an atmosphere of joyous revelation. (Not, however, without the darker notes implicit in the myth of "the golden bough" and in the very phrase "dark eyelids." The reciprocity of the two sections is like that between the male and female principles in Canto 47, much further along—written some dozen years later, in fact, by which time the inseparable association of ecstatic culture-bearing generative power and impersonal, fated destructiveness had become thoroughly worked into the texture of the cantos. It could by that point be evoked by the merest suggestion.) When the romantically resonant names of Helen and Eleanor are introduced early in Canto 2, these figures are presented as destroyers. The scene of Tyro and Poseidon, lyrically exquisite, is nevertheless cold and impersonal, as are the Ileutheria passage just before the canto's end and, farther on, almost the whole of Canto 4. The affect of mingled harshness or coldness and glamorously fixed moments of beautiful ecstasy is brought to a kind of perfection in that canto and echoed at many points throughout the years. One must, naturally, understand that from the viewpoint of lyrical structure these modulations of feeling are—whatever the intellectual or scholarly considerations—the essential stuff in the movement and the music of the poem. A simple way of putting it, but only to start with, is that they project the shifting states of sensibility in the speaker, whatever the literal content.

In any case, once the fixed points of reference to beautiful, deadly, inescapable feminine erotic power are established, the second through seventh cantos develop the Dionysian-phallic energies of the sequence in such a way as both to affirm them and to identify them with the very character of the poet's song. Yet they also acknowledge a fear of being unable to meet the demands of those energies. One catches certain Prufrockian echoes and certain echoes of "Mauberley (1920)." A melancholy, distinctly intimate note is added at the start of Canto 3: "And there were not 'those girls,' there was one face." We have here a perfect instance of the swift precipitating-out of a personal tone from amidst a swarming mass of distracting effects—or, to change the metaphor, its sudden emergence from the thicket of allusion. It enters for a moment, yet gives an unavoidable emotional coloration to the whole canto, the slightest sort of echo of the dark mood of Canto 1, yet unmistakable in its connection with that mood and with the utterly desolate endings of Cantos 3, 4, and 5, the suicidal refrain of Canto 5 ("O se morisse, credesse caduto da sè"—"if he should die, it would be thought he'd killed himself"), and the lament for a lost love in Canto 7. Even the jolly, bawdy quotation from Guillem de Poitiers in lines 4–5 of Canto 6 is preceded by an allusion to the song the sirens sang to Odysseus and followed by a quick association of sexuality and fruitfulness with death:

> The stone is alive in my hand, the crops
> will be thick in my death-year...

The presence of such a personal dimension, however distanced by Pound's method of self-displacement and of distracting our attention—like a lark dropping suddenly and fluttering deceptively at a distance from the nest—is essential in the structuring of a sequence. Not only does it provide the central emotional key in relation to which all the other affective elements operate; it also commits the work to its full task by exposing the underlying emotional issue. The "I" is there, not necessarily in a literal autobiographical sense, although we may be fairly sure that the personal crisis implied is no mere fiction but a source of the work's intensity, turbulence, and psychic self-ravening. It is also crucial to see the other heroic figures of the work in relation to the "I": alternative personae acting out imagined alternative possibilities. The point is not simply, as has so often been suggested, that we have a metamorphic context in which all heroes blend into one another, etc. Abstractly and schematically speaking, the observation is accurate enough. But the emotional point, the artistically relevant point, is the relationship of these personae to the central sensibility.

Thus, as soon as the increasingly personal cycle of Cantos 2–7 is completed, the Malatesta cantos begin and a completely extroverted alternative persona takes over. The Browningesque method becomes very evident in the busyness of these cantos. Interestingly, Pound points to his method by the way he begins Canto 8. He starts by alluding to the crucial psychological confession near the end of "The Waste Land": "These fragments you have shelved (shored)." As if to say, *I, too, but now I'm bringing my fragments out into the open.* And then, enter the world of Sigismundo à la Browning. Yet the canto ends with a reminiscence of its beginning, a view of the fragmented world of Sigismundo at the age of twelve, and of the problem of starting from where you actually are— very much the problem of *The Cantos.* From that world of intense, outward-looking action in an atmosphere as disturbed as our own we move in Canto 12 to the yarns about Baldy Bacon, dos Santos, and the Honest Sailor. These yarns bring us more or less back to our own time; their hard brutality in two instances, and bawdy antisentimentality in the third, are as healthily ironic as

Chaucer. This canto, shaking us out of the spell of Malatesta, is a modulation of tone before we find in Canto 13
that calm wisdom, not unworldly but utterly in control of
the self, whose embodiment is Kung. After which, we
return to the speaker's own world, with all hell literally
breaking loose so that the *Draft of XVI Cantos* ends, as
it began, in the midst of tragic, fateful action, but the
horror now is literal reality, current history.

   This group of cantos stands as a sequence, beautifully,
in the same sense that *The Pisan Cantos* (though far more
poignant in its way) does. The question immediately
rises: What was the effect of issuing Cantos 1–30 as a
group five years later? I believe that the answer lies
mainly in the extraordinarily high frequency in Cantos
17–30 of lyrical extensions of the motifs introduced in the
earlier *Draft*. For example, Canto 17 picks up directly
from the ending of Canto 1, with the words "So that,"
and takes us into the realm of Zagreus and Aphrodite,
the earthly paradise peopled by Homeric divinities and
Renaissance persons. The hero, Odysseus-Pound, is per-
mitted a brief respite by Koré: " 'For this hour, brother
of Circe.' " In this dream-paradise we escape all the
varieties of hell explored in earlier cantos. Again, Canto
20, with its amusing NOIGANDRES passage and its
Ovidian and Odyssean passages, picks up similarly from
Cantos 1 and 2. And Canto 29 reintroduces the Sordello
identification, this time with the intimacy of one who
has suffered the same disillusionment or defeat after
shared love as, supposedly, did Sordello.

   I would like to linger for a moment over the closing
pages of Canto 29. The sexual intimacy here is strikingly
immediate. It begins with the humorous (but at first apparently serious and objective) image: "The mythological
exterior lies on the moss in the forest." Afterwards it
moves into the tenderly insulting love-talk of " 'Nel

ventre tuo, o nelle mente mia,' " and then to the inevitable death-association. All this happens between exquisite lyric passages that provide, first, a quick cosmic distancing, and then a still, calm imagery of impenetrable reality held in stasis by the imagination's power of composition. Canto 29 begins:

> Pearl, great sphere, and hollow,
> Mist over lake, full of sunlight,
> Pernella concubina
> The sleeve green and shot gold over her hand
> Wishing her son to inherit
> Expecting the heir ainé be killed in battle
> He being courageous, poisoned his brother puiné
> Laying blame on Siena

Thus, before we have had time to draw a very deep breath, we have already received an exquisite cosmic image of the sun in mist, an imagist snapshot of Pernella the concubine, a woman involved in a medieval power-intrigue and struggle, and a quick summary of her schemes on behalf of her illegitimate son after her lover's legal heirs have been killed—the younger ("puiné") by poison, the older ("ainé) in battle. The line describing her ("the sleeve green and shot gold over her hand") combines suggestions of desirability, lovely fashionable dress, and a certain aura of unscrupulous purposefulness. The passage has leaped into an atmosphere of turmoil.

The next two stanzas shift, by natural enough associations, to the doings of Sordello's mistress Cunizza da Romano, which Pound recounts with unholy glee. Cunizza's vital, spendthrift presence then takes leave of the poem, making way for two partially allegorical stanzas that are separated by a single line from a randy French folksong. In these stanzas we watch the progress and

overhear the thinking of one "Lusty Juventus," who
moves through the streets of a typical American town. It
is a town of the sort we have come to know in the
writings of such contemporaries of Pound's as Sherwood
Anderson, Sinclair Lewis, and Edgar Lee Masters.

Lusty Juventus, it goes without saying, has a mind of
youth—sensuous, alert, and sardonic toward the older
generation and established attitudes. He also has the
mind of Ezra Pound: a fresh, open intelligence seeking
insights into the universe that will provide a unifying
vision without betraying the demanding reality of par-
ticulars. He moves, that is, responding creatively to the
whole of being. He takes ironic note of the houses he
passes. One belongs to "the funeral director / Whose
daughters' conduct caused comment." Another belongs
to "the amateur student of minerals / That later went
bankrupt." These proprietors are symbolic figures in
their own right, the first embodying a repressive system
of "morality" so moribund it cannot remember its original purposes, the second embodying the prevailing fi-
nancial system. Juventus observes them sharply, while at
the same time delighting himself with metaphysical
speculation:

> "Matter is the lightest of all things,
> Chaff, rolled into balls, tossed, whirled in the aether,
> Undoubtedly crushed by the weight,
> Light also proceeds from the eye;
> In the globe over my head
> Twenty feet in diameter, thirty feet in diameter
> Glassy, the glaring surface—
> There are many reflections
> So that one may watch them turning and moving
> With heads down now, and now up."

All this and so much more! Already we have had every
kind of tone—aesthetic entrancement, Browningesque

speed of action, loving parody of ancient texts, bawdy humor, satirical dismissal—and now comes this meta-physical marveling. The stage has thus been readied for the beautiful play of mind in the concluding part of the poem beginning "The mythological exterior lies on the moss in the forest."

If we isolated that one line, it would be infinitely suggestive. First of all, it seems to present the basic ground of myth, elementary nature, which man then gives magical properties and peoples with his imagination. Secondly, and especially in the context of sexual meditation, the "moss" may even suggest an earth-goddess's presence. These connotations remain, but as we read on we see that the passage presents a dramatic situation with comic elements: a dialogue between Juventus-Pound and a young woman. His fancy plays with the notion that she *is* a goddess, a "mythological exterior" lying with him on the forest floor and—*talking*. It is a scene of innocent intellectual dalliance such as Milton might have envisoned, except that she—"the mythological exterior"—sounds like a very earnest young American woman and he like an ambitious young writer who wants to impress her:

> The mythological exterior lies on the moss in the forest
> And questions him about Darwin.
> And with a burning fire of phantasy
>   he replies with "Deh! nuvoletta..."
> So that she would regret his departure.
>   Drift of weed in the bay:
> She is seeking a guide, a mentor,
> He aspires to a career with honour
> To step in the tracks of his elders;
>   a greater incomprehension?
> There is no greater incomprehension
> Than between the young and the young.

The kaleidoscopic mixture, then, combines a scene of intimate conversation that is basically an effort at communion, awkward and showing off though it may in part be, with the wide prospects of reverie and interior process revealed earlier on. The delighted intelligence that has been darting in so many directions and seeing connections everywhere is now beginning to close in on a few central preoccupations: the process that actually directs the sexual life, the working of male creative intelligence, and the possibility of fixing existence in a timeless, transcendent vision through the aesthetic imagination. These preoccupations combine in the affirmative intelligence that is locating them as the clues to its own surging energy of awareness, the "Molü" that protects the sensibility against the love of death implicit in the panicky, puritanical repression of joy in modern Christian-capitalist civilization.

In this last respect the canto foreshadows the increasingly rich sense of the connection between lively, purposeful intelligence and sexual fatality in such later cantos as 39 and 47. Canto 29, however, is more tentative and less "tragic" than the others. It centers on the sweet proliferations of thought and experience, and on the rich mysteries of desire and mental awakening—

> mind drifts, weed, slow youth, drifts,
> Stretched on the rock, bleached and now floated;
> Wein, Weib, TAN AOIDAN
> Chiefest of these the second, the female
> Is an element, the female
> Is a chaos
> An octopus
> A biological process
> and we seek to fulfill...
> TAN AOIDAN, our desire, drift...
> Ailas e que'm fau miey huelh
> Quar no vezon so qu'ieu vuelh.

> Our mulberry leaf, woman, TAN AOIDAN,
> "Nel ventre tuo, o nella mente mia,
> "Yes, Milady, precisely, if you wd.
> have anything properly made."
>
> "Faziamo tutte le due...
> "No, not in the palm-room." The lady says it is
> Too cold in the palm-room. . . ."

Here is the speaker's (decidedly male) mind playing with the stuff of life and consciousness. The luxury of it overcomes him—"wine, woman, song." But as he is a *mind* and not just a tuning fork set vibrating, he extends the linguistic connotations of the phrase. He recalls its original form, perhaps even to bring Luther—who composed the jolly little song to begin with—into the range of the poem: a neglected aspect of the Lutheran tradition, so to speak. The Greek phrase for "song" is added, with the result that in "Wein, Weib, TAN AOIDAN" the hedonistic drift has been conditioned by classical and religious cultural sets of European tradition. The half-facetious terms for "the female" are equally conditioned by the larger context of thought. To the male mind, bewildered, desiring, and entrapped by sexual compulsion, she may be chaos, octopus, and biological process all at once (and besides, the words provide a splendidly bemusing group of internal rhymes), but she is also the force that draws even a Luther into action. I don't mean to be solemn; you may be sure Pound isn't. It's simply that his mind is racing ecstatically along, entranced by the connections of thought and image and sound. When he brings in Sordello's Provençal couplet ("Alas, that my eyes are no use to me / For they don't see what I wish to see"), we are in the earthily Platonic troubadour tradition, echoed in the Italian address to the lady that follows: "In your womb, or in my mind." And he proposes: "Let's activate (do) both." But no, it's too cold, she protests—the fantasy continuing.

The canto ends with the timeless vision mentioned earlier, of impenetrable reality. Having flung himself into the hubbub of Sordello's world at the start of the canto, and then into the world of his mental dance, including the excitement of sexual arousal and its intellectual permutations, the speaker now distances himself with a mosaic of images that taken together compose a calm center of transcendent awareness. These are images comparable with those that have been dancing before us hitherto, but they are marked by stillness rather than activity. The aesthetic now is not of process but of achieved form or presence. We are back in the realm of the poem's opening image ("Pearl, great sphere, and hollow") before the mind's furious energy began running riot. Everything is in sharp outline; the word "clear" dominates:

> The tower, ivory, the clear sky
> Ivory rigid in sunlight
> And the pale clear of the heaven
> Phoibos of narrow thighs,
> The cut cool of the air . . .

Pictures stand out sharply: a peasant girl ("Beauty on an ass-cart / Sitting on five sacks of laundry"), Venice at night ("Glide of water, lights and the prore, / Silver beaks out of night"), the trees fading out ("melted in air") as darkness takes over and the distancing is completed.

This distancing prefigures the Artemis canto, which closes *A Draft of XXX Cantos*, with its beautiful antisentimental opening—

> Compleynt, compleynt I hearde upon a day,
> Artemis singing, Artemis, Artemis
> Agaynst Pity lifted her wail—

and with its reprise of earlier motifs and its whole classic elegiac balance. The addition of Cantos 17–30 has
made a *A Draft of XXX Cantos* less contrived in structure
than the first sixteen were when published by themselves as a unit. Pound's method of proliferation, of ex-
pansion and then sharply oriented focusing such as we
have just seen in Canto 29, has come into its own. Adding the new cantos has softened the perhaps too sharply
delineated outlines of the earlier group without disturbing its centers of gravity.

With *Eleven New Cantos XXXI–XLI* (1934) the centers of
gravity do shift. Despite certain continuities, this volume and the two succeeding ones, *The Fifth Decad of
Cantos XLII–LI* (1937) and *Cantos LII–LXXI* (1940), move
into an atmosphere of tendentious rhetoric doubtless
foreshadowed in *A Draft of XXX Cantos* but present, for
one thing, in greater proportion than before. The curve
of movement in *Eleven New Cantos* is from the exaltation
of Jefferson and Adams (alternative personae, "thrones")
to the exaltation of Mussolini (ditto), rather than from
The Book of the Dead, with Odysseus at its center, to the
contemporary realm of death, with all of us at the center.
Cantos 36 and 39, which carry the lyric burden, are the
chief links with the resonant centers of passionate and
visionary intensity earlier on. They lend poetic "authority" to the rhetorical, political, and history-wise voices
that dominate the group. (Pound is continuing with the
technique that worked so well in Cantos 17–30. Now,
however, it seems more mechanical than organic—not
that the two cantos are not splendid in themselves.) A
new voyager-figure, Hanno, the Carthaginian, is introduced at the end of Canto 40. The style grows taut
and direct now, an admirable adaptation to poetic form
of an essentially documentary, matter-of-fact historical
source. It suggests the no-nonsense, practical genius of

Hanno as he proceeded to accomplish necessary tasks despite the ignorance and stupidity all around him. Wedged between the polemic at the start of Canto 40 against war-profiteering and the money system, and the introduction of Mussolini's comparable talents and achievements at the beginning of the next canto, the Hanno passage gives historical depth and a neutral tone to the building up of Mussolini as an equivalent to the American founding fathers.

Here, of course, with their anti-Semitism and blatant Fascist propaganda, *The Cantos* made even more trouble for themselves than the scurrilous hell-cantos had done. Homer, Dante, Sordello, Cavalcanti—and even Adams and Jefferson—have authority by definition. They invite our openness to the splendors and the humanity of their qualities which the poem may unfold. With Mussolini, at least some of us will feel very much as Christians being fed to the lions might once have felt about the glory of Rome. Pound certainly tests the limits of our moral empathy here, as he will do again at the start of *The Pisan Cantos* and elsewhere.

Be all that as it may, I should like to note here that Pound's genius in deploying documentary quotations and other data is extraordinary. He does lose aesthetic perspective and grow lengthy because of his love of the materials and of the sound of the human voice expressing, however drily and repetitiously, certain favorite doctrines that seem to him hard, vibrantly relevant kernels of perception. But he also makes a found poetry of these materials—rearranges them, creates internal rhymes, balances them against snatches of his own phrasing and pure imagistic flashes or other quick poetic notations. The intrinsic poetics of expository speech created a special music for him, so that a phrase like "every bank of discount" becomes a refrain in a lyrical sense, not merely a reiterated point of argument. One has only to compare his use of such materials with that of certain of his followers—Charles Olson, for instance—to see how much truer his ear is than theirs. Line by line he is superb, although page by page one does grow a bit weary.

Still, it is interesting that in these volumes written in the 1930s the passionate lyric centers, harking back to early work and usually based on the *Odyssey*, are indispensable. Each volume introduces a new set of supposed intellectually compelling referents—the founding fathers, Martin Van Buren, Mussolini, and others in 1934; the Monte dei Paschi and Japanese and Chinese culture in 1937; Chinese history in 1940. The new materials carry with them different formal modes of giving new body and emotional force—the idiom of song, the sense of concrete realities—to much-repeated political and economic ideas. But it is not until *The Pisan Cantos* (1948) that we again have a group of intrinsic poetic authority in the same sense as *A Draft of XVI Cantos* or *A Draft of XXX Cantos*—this despite the fact that *The Pisan Cantos* begins with its outrageous deification of Mussolini and a dogged insistence on the rightness of the Fascist cause.

The reason is simple. From the opening line on, the sequence is charged with a new kind of tragic feeling. It is anchored in the life and suggestiveness of the language and the authenticity of personal circumstance of the speaker—not so much now a madly exacerbated polemicist as a kind of victim-voyager caught amid squalid trappings and in the most direct, earthy, and inescapable contact with the prison-camp world. We don't really care what Odysseus's political opinions were—actually, he was a murdering absolute ruler if there ever was one—and we wouldn't want Homer to harangue us on page after page with those opinions. If *The Cantos* do constitute a single sequence in any useful sense, we would have to say they culminated in *The Pisan Cantos*. For in this sequence the form realizes itself more than in the others. The protagonist regains his full authority after being brought down. He endures the symbolic death that has always been on his mind and accepts disastrous isolation and deprivation in a new way, while echoing his earlier self enough to make the new perspectives absolutely continuous with his memory and his enduring preoccupations.

The dynamics of *The Pisan Cantos* are superbly realized, from the complex balancing of all the major motifs and tones in the long prelude that is Canto 74 to their compressed reprise in Canto 84, with its almost plaintive assertion:

> Under white clouds, cielo di Pisa
> out of all this beauty something must come . . .

In these poems, we see, his "burning fire of phantasy" has remained with the poet from the days of his young manhood described in Canto 29. It has flared up again after the shock of the defeat of Italy and of Pound's imprisonment by the United States Army in Italy shortly afterwards. The literal man himself is present as never before, enduring the passage—or rather, the stagnation—of time, keeping sane, remembering past places and experiences, counting and identifying birds that light on wires as a kind of refrain or rhythmic marker during the long days. One could easily devote a long book to these eleven cantos. Here I wish to note only a few special considerations, mostly evidenced in the first poem, Canto 74.

At the most elementary level, we have one reality: the poet's physical hardship and deprivation in the detention camp. The fact that he is an aging man in brutal cir-

cumstances is a basic fact of the sequence. So is the presence of the prison-guards and of his fellow-prisoners.
These facts make themselves felt in many ways. Yet they
are almost never described or even mentioned. The following passages are among the very few that *approach*
specific reference to them:

> lay there Barabbas and two thieves lay beside him
> infantile synthesis in Barabbas
> minus Hemingway, minus Antheil . . .
>
> (Canto 74)
>
> and they digged a ditch round about me
> lest the damp gnaw thru my bones
>
> (Canto 74)
>
> Tard, très tard je t'ai connue, la Tristesse,
> I have been hard as youth sixty years
>
> (Canto 80)
>
> men of no fortune and with a name to come
>
> his helmet is used for a pisspot
> this helmet is used for my footbath
>
> (Canto 80)
>
> If the hoar frost grip thy tent
> Thou wilt give thanks when night is spent.
>
> (Canto 84)

These passages are the closest the speaker gets to anything like a complaint about the grim life in the Detention Training Center north of Pisa where Pound was
kept for six months in 1945. The other men there with
him were charged with violent crimes such as rape and
murder. Pound was at first put into one of the outdoor
"cages," each just over six feet square, where men were
exposed to the elements and to a great deal of dust. "In
about three weeks he collapsed: claustrophobia, partial
amnesia, bouts of hysteria and terror. . . . They moved

him to a tent in the Medical Compound."* It is striking
that the cantos themselves avoid reporting this ordeal or
even the circumstances that would lead to it. We get only
such flashes as I have cited and a few implied confes-
sions of anguish such as this one in Canto 83:

> When the mind swings by a grass-blade
> an ant's forefoot shall save you

   In general, Pound's allusions to the DTC, though de-
tailed and full of robust interest in the speech of the
other prisoners, are restrained about his own situation.
At the same time, stark melancholy does prevail. The
sense of loneliness and nostalgia, and of being reduced
to nonentity, is the major ambience of the sequence. The
speaker combats it with the sheer vigor of his ever-ac-
tive, concretely attentive mind. He has a saving humor;
he wards off self-pity by thinking in metaphor, in echoes
of the speech and writing of others, and in associative
clusters of memories; and he takes the offensive against
his present predicament by placing it in historical and
political perspective—according to his lights, of course.
But the whole work is nonetheless saturated with a desperate melancholy. Even in the passages I have cited as
referring in some degree to physical and psychological
suffering explicitly connected with conditions in the
DTC, the dominant quality of the affect derives mainly
from this deep feeling of displacement and free-floating
unhappiness. The passages from Canto 80, for instance,
echo Pound's beloved Villon and Homer to convey his
mood without bathos but with enormous emphasis.
Even so, he takes any curse of mere lugubriousness away
from these echoings. He follows the first one with a line

---

*Hugh Kenner, *The Pound Era* (Berkeley and Los Angeles: University of Cali-
fornia Press, 1971), pp. 462–63.

of subtle self-criticism ("I have been hard as youth sixty years"), in which "hard" rhymes with the repeated "tard" of the preceding line—another self-critical note— and thus distracts attention from the definitive "Tristesse." In the same way, the line from the *Odyssey* ("men of no fortune and with a name to come"—the epitaph for the pathetic young Elpenor, altered to the plural to characterize Pound and his fellow-prisoners) is followed by two lines of earthy song. These lines suggest prison squalor, but with a certain cheeriness, and Pound exercises his poet's wit on the internal rhymes of "his helmet," "pisspot," and "this helmet" and on the hearty trochaic echoing of "pisspot" and "footbath." Yet it is the essential sadness of the phrasing from Villon and from Homer that gives each passage its emotional coloring. Pound cannot help putting his misery with a certain style. He asserts himself even while confiding his helplessness, as in Canto 76:

> As a lone ant from a broken ant-hill
> from the wreckage of Europe, ego scriptor.

A number of sections of *The Pisan Cantos* that at first seem merely outpourings of proliferative association—internally fascinating and ingenious, it may be, and yet overly copious—reveal their true poetic relevance when read in the light of this slightly masked spiritual despair. Fairly early in Canto 74, for instance, we come upon a passage in which the speaker is recalling Odysseus's reply when the Cyclops demanded his name: "ΟΫ ΤΙΣ" ("No Man")—

> ΟΫ ΤΙΣ, ΟΫ ΤΙΣ? Odysseus
> the name of my family.
> the wind also is of the process . . .

The speaker too is "no man," a wanderer like Odysseus wherever the winds carry him, and an "odious" outcast

(by association with the etymology of the name "Odysseus," with archaic suggestions of the hero as a sacrificial scapegoat and taboo-figure). With outward calm, the
speaker here submits to an erosive destiny that reduces
him to nothingness, his supposed mission forever
stalled, his very name obliterated.

Later in the same canto we have a longer passage with
a typically diffuse surface that, if we are sufficiently attentive, discloses the painful nostalgia motivating it.
Pound has internalized myriad touchstones of memory
from "the wreckage of Europe," and of himself, and he is
virtually certain that he will never again be free to have
such experiences. In the grain of this passage, its fresh
recollection that has all the immediacy of direct impact
except—disastrous exception!—the literal touch of reality, lives the intrinsically tragic melody of these cantos.

el triste pensier si volge
        ad Ussel. A Ventadour
                va il consire, el tempo rivolge
and at Limoges the young salesman
bowed with such French politeness "No that is impossible."
I have forgotten which city
But the caverns are less enchanting to the unskilled explorer
        than the Urochs as shown on the postals,
we will see those old roads again, question,
                                possibly
but nothing appears much less likely,
                        Mme Pujol . . .

The passage comes after a series of lines giving a
rather bleak closeup of the camp (except for one line,
"Butterflies, mint and Lesbia's sparrows," that shows
Pound's mind and senses open to whatever happy impression may come along). His memory-filled imagination comes to the poet's rescue and "the sad thought
turns toward Ussel. Toward Ventadour his attention

goes. Time turns back." The modified Dantean form and the feeling of heavy sorrow in "el triste pensier" allow Pound to project in Italian a mood he seldom permits himself to indulge in straightforward English. The passage is filled with memories of people and places once encountered in southern France, including caverns with paleolithic paintings on the walls. The precise mental state of the remembered moments comes back as it was—a certain disappointment in the caverns, for example, and the manner of a young French salesman. The feeling of irrevocable loss, and of frayed hopes, comes through with absolute spontaneity in the lines "we will see those old roads again, question / possibly / but nothing appears much less likely"—lines that are no less touching for their diffident tentativeness. At the end the unfocused words "Mme Pujol" keep the atmosphere tenuous and desolate, an ambiguity there is no point in pursuing.

Something rather marvelous, poetically, happens immediately after this passage. The atmosphere of reminiscence is transferred to the present scene: that is, to the prison-camp and its environs. We were perhaps being somewhat readied for this turn by the one "happy impression" of the camp I have already mentioned. Suddenly now the prisoners' world is transformed into a series of pastoral impressions, as if remembered from another time. The images have a calm stillness as of beautiful moments of awareness. Only one line, "A lizard upheld me," suggests that the speaker needed to concentrate on such tiny realities to keep himself under control (as in "an ant's forefoot shall save you"). At the end he experiences a moment of blissful transcendence as poignant in its way, given his circumstances, as the flash of memory was in the preceding passage. "Kuanon," the Chinese goddess of mercy, graces him

with this moment of epiphany, for he has been imagin-
ing to himself that one of the mountains visible from the
camp is Mount Taishan, the sacred mountain in West
Shantung Province. (We will remember the gift of Molü,
in Canto 47, which enables the creative imagination to
triumph, within the limits of mortality, over the base
and bestial aspects of existence.)

> and there was a smell of mint under the tent flaps
> especially after the rain
>   and a white ox on the road toward Pisa
>   as if facing the tower,
> dark sheep in the drill field and on wet days were clouds
> in the mountain as if under the guard roosts.
>   A lizard upheld me
>   the wild birds wd not eat the white bread
>   from Mt. Taishan to the sunset
> From Carrara stone to the tower
>   and this day the air was made open
>   for Kuanon of all delights . . .

The intensity of such transcendent passages in these
cantos is that of poised instants of clarity within highly
volatile states, in which terror and joy become reciprocals of one another. Another instance is the music of
birds, the "song out of Phlegethon," of Canto 75. Another is the lyric moment beginning with a line from
Dante when Aphrodite's eyes appear ("there came new
subtlety of eyes into my tent"). This is in Canto 81, and
the moment blends into the most famous passage in *The
Pisan Cantos* ("What thou lovest well remains . . ."), in
which the speaker astringently preaches humility to
himself but still affirms the value of the risks he has
taken as a man and as an artist. I shall note here only one
more instance, the love-poem to earth and death in
Canto 86. In this passage as in Whitman's "Out of the
Cradle Endlessly Rocking"—to which Pound alludes ex-

plicitly—a deeply depressed sense of "the loneliness of death" is absorbed into an exquisite music of ultimately sexual self-immolation foreshadowed in Canto 47.

I have so far scanted the political aspect of *The Pisan Cantos* in order to stress its tragic bearing and qualities of structure. But because the political aspect is part of the structure, the tragic element has its impure dimension. There is no problem if we think of the work as the expression of genius under duress: the predicament of the sturdy, weatherbeaten poet finding himself in a prison-camp after the war. "A lone ant from a broken ant-hill / from the wreckage of Europe," he endures his trials stoically, makes the best artistic use of his experience, and goes on with his highly charged inner life at full speed. In fact, he does so more magnificently than ever because of his adversity.

Obviously, there is another side to it all. It is suggested very tangentially in a quotation I have already given:

> Lay there Barabbas and two thieves lay beside him
> infantile synthesis in Barabbas
> minus Hemingway, minus Antheil . . .

In these lines Pound comes closest to presenting himself as a martyr, although he slips out from under any such assertion slyly. In the Gospels Jesus is described as being between two thieves on the Cross; but Pound omits the Cross and substitutes Barabbas the failed revolutionist, whose release the people demanded instead of Christ's. A minor but significant Biblical figure, Barabbas serves as a secular, political alternative to Christ. Pilate spared him, while Jesus suffered the Crucifixion. Pound, without books or music (Hemingway, Antheil), in the company of accused criminals, but after all still alive, embodies the "infantile synthesis" at the other end of the scale from genuine martyrdom or the self-transcendence through death and rebirth of a Jesus or Dionysus.

The true martyr, Pound proposes at the very start of *The Pisan Cantos*, is Mussolini the "twice crucified." Pound's sufferings are only incidental to the major tragedy, the downfall of the Fascist regime. Such is the viewpoint implied in the resounding opening lines of Canto 74 that set the emotional stage for the Pisan group. The fall of Mussolini is introduced in the context of an enormously compassionate image of thwarted human aspirations. The whole opening is an audacious challenge directed against the winning forces in World War II.

The enormous tragedy of the dream in the peasant's bent
    shoulders
Manes! Manes was tanned and stuffed,
Thus Ben and la Clara *a Milano*
            by the heels at Milano
That maggots shd/eat the dead bullock
DIGONOS, Δίγονος, but the twice crucified
                where in history will you find it?
yet say this to the Possum: a bang, not a whimper,
        with a bang not with a whimper,
To build the city of Dioce whose terraces are the colour of
    stars.

The noble, Hugoesque first line is immediately followed by lines that idealize Benito Mussolini (lynched in Milan together with his mistress, Clara Petacci) as the embodiment of the great humane dream of peasant emancipation. The shout "Manes!" is a remote echo of "Tamuz!" in Canto 47. "Ben" is a manes now—a shade to be revered and avenged. He is compared with Dionysus, whose epithet was *"digonos"*: "twice born." The difference lies in Mussolini's having been "twice crucified" instead, first by defeat in war and then by murder, but this phrase only reinforces the symbolic deification. Un-

like the "hollow men" of Eliot's poem, he died with "a
bang, not a whimper." The implication is that Pound in-
tends to do the same and is defiantly sending this message to his old friend ("the Possum"), who would hardly
agree with his estimate of the Mussolini regime. Mussolini's dream, shared by Pound, is reflected in the image
of Dioce (Ecbatana) that recurs in this group of cantos. It
is the dream of building a world as prosperous and
beautiful as that ancient city, described by Herodotus in
language that Pound follows.

The passage is not all nobility; it also hisses vitupera-
tively. It vilifies the partisans in Milan and the people
who "betrayed" the dead ruler and violated the supposed meaning of his presence. Granted that the poem's
hatred of Fascism's enemies, like its exaltation of *il Duce*,
is a terrible evidence of Pound's distorted political values. To lavish such love and admiration on so despicable
a tyrant is unthinkable, objectively speaking. Still, the
first line in the quotation is perfectly genuine in its reverberating humanity, as is the final line in its evocation
of the fabulous community of our dreams. Nor are the
lines in between any the less authentic in the passionate
indignation and private commitment they express. Un-
palatable as it may be, the handling of language here, in
which magnanimous vision is combined with embittered resentment and with staunch loyalty, makes for
superb political poetry. Change the names and a few
specific details, and the same passage could be used to
memorialize a political martyrdom or defeat in a cause
cherished by more of us—that of Martin Luther King, for
instance. Political emotion of this sort derives not from
the rightness but from the conviction and sense of
shared purpose and sacrifice of the speaker.

From this stormy beginning Canto 74 progresses
through several phases. The combined elegy and paean

for Mussolini is supported in later passages that assail
the "usurious" banking systems and the governments of
the Allies and the influence of Jews. Meanwhile, we
have seen, a counter-music to that of political and economic rhetoric is established as well. It is the music of
personal memory and longing, of the presence of a man's
whole empirical past in his mind in the midst of confine-
ment and loss. The opening passage I have been discussing has this private music in it as well as its rhetorical
melody. The language of great, disappointed dreams and
of anger in defeat has its purely subjective dimension.
The passage is succeeded by a more lyrical one whose
tone and images are of the fatalistic acceptance of inevitable "process" and loss:

> The suave eyes, quiet, not scornful,
>
> rain also is of the process.
> What you depart from is not the way
> and olive tree blown white in the wind
> washed in the Kiang and Han
> what whiteness will you add to this whiteness,
>
> what candor?

After the reference to Dioce the scope of allusion has
grown worldwide and the sting of defeat in war and personal disaster has been absorbed into a kind of reconciliation to the universal process of change. The image of
"the suave eyes" is related to this reconciliation; it is associated with Aphrodite, goddess of the life-process to
which the whole of *The Cantos* pays obeisance. In context, though, this image seems also to continue the ideal-
ization of Mussolini, suggesting his heroic posture of
calm transcendence. And the speaker may well be re-
minding himself of the "suavity" needed to control one's
excitement by distancing it, an implied comparison with

Odysseus (whose voyages and name are brought into the poem a bit further on).

Just because they are so magnetically engaging in their art and in the richness with which they project their protagonist's situation and extraordinary sensibility, *The Pisan Cantos* confront us even more than the earlier groups of cantos do with a dilemma of sympathy. By their nature they forbid us to read them apolitically, and we shall do best if we see them for what they are—a tremendously moving work warped by a vileness whose peculiar vehement music is an essential element in their movement along with the other emotional components. Certainly it does no good to pretend the vileness is not there. One must be prepared to take a work of genius for what it is, seeing in its formations the surprising possibilities of the human spirit.

The politics of *The Pisan Cantos,* despite what I have called the vileness, is hardly simple. It is a mixture that includes a good deal of humane and even pacifist feeling, as witness the very first line: "The enormous tragedy of the dream in the peasant's bent shoulders," or the endings of Cantos 76 and 78:

> woe to them that conquer with armies
> and whose only right is their power

and

> there
> are
> no
> righteous
> wars

Canto 80 balances pain on behalf of "poor old Benito" against a subtle perception of one of the chief problems of political idealism:

> the problem after any revolution is what to do with
> your gunmen
> as old Billyum found out in Oireland
>   in the Senate, Bedad! or before then
>   Your gunmen thread on moi drreams
>   O woman shapely as a swan,
> Your gunmen tread on my dreams

In slightly different form this was the problem that broke
on Yeats ("old Billyum") in "Meditations in Time of
Civil War." One might argue that all this humanistic
side of Pound's political intelligence is mere disgruntle-
ment in the wake of the defeat of the Fascist government
in the war, but that would be unjust. The war-poems in
Mauberley alone would contradict such a thought.
Pound's attitude toward his fellow-prisoners, a fair
number of whom were black, is sympathetic and appre-
ciative throughout these cantos. And of course his own
imprisonment brought certain kinds of injustice home to
him:

> Nor can who has passed a month in the death cells
>   believe in capital punishment
> No man who has passed a month in the death cells
>   believes in cages for beasts
>
>   (Canto 83)

These four small passages reflect as many tones:
prophecy, manifesto, exquisite buffoonery shot through
with romantic echoes of Yeats, and dourly compassionate rhetoric. The sequence is saturated with varied
political tonalities. The emotional life of these cantos is
very much engaged with them, and in general the dynamics of the Pisan group involves a movement from
more violent to more gentle political expression, as with
the movement of the more personal feeling. Thus, we
have the difference between the drastic image for the

speaker's personal situation that ends Canto 74 and the restrained, stoical one that ends Canto 84. The difference is a reflex of the drift toward acceptance of a humbled state without surrender of self-regard.

> Hast'ou seen the rose in the steel dust
> (or swansdown ever?)
> so light is the urging, so ordered the dark petals of iron
> we who have passed over Lethe.
>
> (Canto 74)

> If the hoar frost grip thy tent
> Thou wilt give thanks when night is spent.
>
> (Canto 84)

Within this general drift, or sifting, of feeling in *The Pisan Cantos* we find the usual swirling surface with its multiple sparks of wit and feeling. The cantos fall into three main groupings that overlap and refuse to stay absolutely still for analysis as they surge and eddy and form their involved, knotty patterns on their way to such tranquility as they can muster. The first grouping, Cantos 74–77, is built around the juxtapositions of Canto 74 I have described. These cantos present the speaker—artist, political idealist (according to his lights), and Confucian thinker—in his symbolic hell. (Canto 75 is a musical correlative for his song that rises "out of Phlegethon." It is mostly a musical score of a chorus of birds by Clement Janequin, transcribed for modern violin performance by Gerhardt Münch.* *The Cantos,* incidentally, are filled with bird-imagery closely related to the protagonist's psychic states.)

The second grouping, Cantos 78–82, isolates and refocuses the major directions of feeling suggested in the welter of motifs that the previous four cantos have introduced. Canto 78 centers on Pound's bitter hostility

*See Ezra Pound, *ABC of Reading* (New York: New Directions, 1960), p. 54.

toward war and its economic causes. Canto 79 swells into a beautiful celebration of fruitfulness and love, with an invocation to the "Lynx" as the magical beast sacred to Aphrodite and guardian of the ripe perfection of the life process. Then Canto 80, at the center of the Pisan group, emerges, almost as long as the twenty-five-page Canto 74 and equally proliferative of motifs. But it too, like the preceding pair of cantos, simplifies by isolating a definitive tone of the sequence; it is almost entirely elegiac. "Senesco sed amo"—"I grow old but I love"—is a minor but persistent note in this subtle exploration of nostalgic efforts to repossess a lost past that continues to compel our imaginations. Cantos 81 and 82 then pick up the more concentrated focusing of Cantos 78 and 79 and provide the climactic music of *The Pisan Cantos*. Canto 81 passes through several lyric phases rapidly, reaching a moment of pure vision followed by the poet's self-transcendent dialogue with himself at the end. Canto 82, more darkly intense, confronts the terror of the speaker's whole predicament and the reality of death. Cantos 84 and 85 are the third grouping, providing a kind of denouement; these are the relatively gentle cantos of relative reconciliation, holding firm and yet letting up on the more aggressive forms of intensity.

Among so many passages I might single out for attention, I should like to point to the endings of the two climactic cantos—the passage beginning "What thou lovest well remains" in Canto 81 and the shorter one beginning "strong as the undertow / of the wave receding" in Canto 82. The former passage comes into view blazingly after a series of moving effects. It is very early morning in the DTC as Canto 81 begins; and the poet's morale is at a high pitch, as the opening lines show:

> Zeus lies in Ceres' bosom
> Taishan is attended of loves
>   under Cythera, before sunrise

Presumably the morning star is clearly visible, and
Venus ("Cythera") has sent the poet's imagination soaring. His mind then goes careening among personal
memories, anecdotes that have been recounted to him,
and snatches from his reading until he suddenly re-
members—probably because he has remembered Love-
lace's poem "To Althea from Prison"—where he is now:

> AOI!
> a leaf in the current
> > at my grates no Althea

A song for which Pound gives us the "libretto" follows,
a lullaby to himself in the name of music and beautifully
fashioned instruments. After it comes the vision of
Aphrodite's "eyes and stance between the eyes" in his
tent—"shone from the unmasked eyes in half-mask's
space." Although he has been so totally dispossessed, he
has this essential vision still: "What thou lovest well
remains." From here on the song is one of self-confron-
tation. He reassures himself that what he "loves well"
cannot be taken from him—then castigates his own vanity in order to be in readiness for a kind of secular grace.
The final lines are blissful, a full recovery of self-regard
as he recounts his own acts that he loveth well and that
therefore remain:

> But to have done instead of not doing
> > this is not vanity
> To have, with decency, knocked
> That a Blunt should open
> > To have gathered from the air a live tradition
> or from a fine old eye the unconquered flame
> This is not vanity.
> > Here error is all in the not done,
> all in the diffidence that faltered . . .

It is not vanity, after a career such as Pound's, to recall
with satisfaction how he paid his respects to a worthy

older poet (Wilfrid Scawen Blunt) and to connect that act
with his own effort to grasp and carry forward the "live
tradition." The affect here is a complex one, with elements of a restrained pride of accomplishment and of the
inescapable pressure to make that effort—to "give a
shout without delay" and leap into the heroic, uncertain
task, like Odysseus in Canto 47.

Canto 82 is emotionally reciprocal with this orientation: it faces the consequences. As before, Pound goes
through a preliminary warming-up process involving
personal reminiscence and consciousness of living history. In these two cantos he is in a deeply confessional
mood, and because death is weighing on his mind it is
natural for him to apostrophize Whitman and quote from
"Out of the Cradle Endlessly Rocking." Tension in-
creases while we wait out a digression on the burial of a
fifteenth-century ruler. And then the ending:

                              strong as the undertow
          of the wave receding
but that a man should live in that further terror, and live
          the loneliness of death came upon me
          (at 3 P. M., for an instant)   δακρύων
                                                  ἐντεῦθεῖ
three solemn half notes
          their white downy chests black-rimmed
on the middle wire
                    periplum

This is a desolation and anxiety beyond ordinary fear
of death. The question arises: Do the birds and their
song embody the terror or are they a sanity-sustaining
life-reminder? Probably the latter; the word "periplum"
suggests this, for the birds are points of reference in a
continuing voyage. The resolutions and balances of
Cantos 81 and 82 are the basic ones of the sequence; they

are fundamental yet tentative, like the two juxtaposed Greek words for "weeping" and for "thence."

The Cantos is a jungle that nevertheless has its clear phases and divisions. I have tried to suggest the sorts of consideration that a fully adequate evaluative examination of its structure would entail, but in the process I have had to ignore many fascinating aspects and even the three final volumes, *Rock-Drill de los Cantares LXXXV–XCV* (1955), *Thrones de los Cantares XCVI–CIX* (1959), and *Drafts and Fragments of Cantos CX–CXVII* (1969). They present dazzling passages, often in new keys, and in their fashion serve an artistic role similar to that of Cantos 17–30 in relation to Cantos 1–16. They displace any sense of a continuing autobiographical perspective and cast a final glow of golden, impersonal light. At one time we thought the final structure would parallel that of *The Divine Comedy* or perhaps of the *Odyssey* or both. Now it has long become clear that *The Cantos* allude significantly to those models and their structures but do not follow them at all systematically. Pound's mind teemed with phrases, images, and figures from myth and literature, and from his own experiences. They were at once fixed points of reference and energizers of the associative, improvisational process always at work in his writing. He did not forget impressions or tones of any kind readily. Taken all together, they exerted a constant pressure on him, similar in kind to that exerted by the insistent dead on Odysseus—too much to handle very neatly except in a single poem or passage, yet powerfully mobilized toward the emotional and visionary balance that was the object of his poetic journey.

Chapter 6

Yeats the Modern Lyric Poet:
AROUND *THE TOWER*

I have half-meant to indulge myself, in this chapter, in a sort of polemic. It would be directed against the non-poetic treatment of Yeats by so many critics—thoughtful and learned critics (of course), Hibernophiliac critics, Maud-Gonneomanic critics, critics who plunge into chthonic mysteries and to whom poems are "but wandering holes" stuffed with bits of Gnostic wadding, and critics who begin books called *Yeats* by citing Dr. Johnson and end them by citing Martin Buber and who instruct the poet in just what philosophical positions and poetic influences he should or should not have harkened to.

But the very thought is like a knell, glazing o'er my glow of noble exasperation, to toll me back to my sole theme: poems. William Butler Yeats was the man who wrote, for instance, the following poem:

MEMORY
One had a lovely face,
And two or three had charm,

> But charm and face were in vain
> Because the mountain grass
> Cannot but keep the form
> Where the mountain hare has lain.

"Memory" is surely one of Yeats's more direct and concentrated successes. Its quality is rooted in its apparently simple yet gristly, tensile form. It is a single sentence in which each line grafts a new perspective onto the poem's increasingly physical statement. Even the rhyme-scheme has this organic character of complex life within the uncomplicated exterior. Three lines apart, the rhymes are sufficiently delayed to avoid any suggestion of the facile. Until the last rhyme, which clicks the poem shut, they are inexact. The iambic trimeter lines, meanwhile, are deftly varied so that the subtle displacements of accent actually syncopate the rhythm. The only marked pauses occur after the first and second lines; thereafter rhyme and meter are put to the service of the one sweep of passionate assertion that culminates in the metaphor of mountain hare and mountain grass.

That culminating metaphor lifts the poem away from affectation or sentimentality. Although the first half of the poem, both through its tone and through explicit statement—"charm and face were in vain"—has already dismissed superficial feminine attractiveness, the second half clinches the case with its earthy image of the permanent impact of one life upon another. It is an image of animal intimacy, without genteel "delicacy" and yet without bawdiness either, and it has as much to say about spiritual as about bodily magnetism. It is like the love-talk in *The Cantos* but concerns a lost love rather than one gratifyingly in progress. Despite its brevity, we cannot quite think of "Memory" as a slight poem. It illustrates Yeats's special genius, his gift for using his great virtuosity to arrive at moments of powerful emotional discovery: elemental moments of confessional force in their clear, hard intensity. In them are revealed the design and direction of a poem beyond its elegances of word-play and intricacies of sound and its display, however subtle or profound and intellectually impressive, of moral or philosophical positions.

Such a moment is the one that comes at the end of the climactic third stanza of "Sailing to Byzantium," in which the speaker reveals how, as his old age approaches, he is lashed by tormenting desire for the passionate life of his youth.

> Consume my heart away; sick with desire
> And fastened to a dying animal
> It knows not what it is . . .

Here, at the core of "Sailing to Byzantium," we see the same possession by an imperious past as in "Memory." But in this poem the speaker tries to wrench himself away from that bondage—or rather, he purports to be trying to do so. In the final stanza he projects a counter-music of self-transcendence to replace the sensual music of sexuality. Yet its whole function is only to manage a kind of control or distancing of his desire to be part of the "country" of sexually enmeshed existence in which his "heart," as the third stanza has told us, still lives. The poem is a rich little system, with its world of ardent entrancement in the first stanza, its yearning in the second stanza for an ecstasy beyond the flesh in which the soul can "clap its hands and sing, and louder sing / For every tatter in its mortal dress," its desperate plea in the third to "sages standing in God's holy fire" to burn away his desiring heart, and its concluding dream of cool, timeless Byzantine perfection. But the two and a half lines I have quoted from the third stanza define the furthest pitch of intensity in the poem and therefore dominate its structure. The gaiety of the image of the soul clapping its hands and singing, the insistent imperative force of the prayer to the sages, and the vision of tranquility attained by the sacrifice of love's urgencies depend on those lines for their own vitality—they are reflexes of the suffering and helplessness and confusion discovered in the climactic phrasing.

Both "Memory" and "Sailing to Byzantium" are instances of Yeats's mature lyric poetry. "Memory" is mature poetry in the most basic sense, for its language is the fruit of a lifetime of experience reported *within* the poem. Long after lovers have parted for good, the man's deepest self still belongs to the woman, the "mountain hare" for whom he was the "mountain grass." These metaphors reverse the roles of the sexes, but this fact does not matter given the quality and the reciprocities of feeling implied. Nor does it matter that in nature the hollow left in the grass by an animal's body would soon enough vanish; in the realm of feeling the impression remains forever alive and profound, and the loss retains its sting of immediacy. The images of mountain hare and mountain grass make an impersonal energy of private memory. The fine virtuosity, the music, of the poem is a rhythmically climactic realization of the continuous ache of irreparable loss. The "dying animal" figure at the height of "Sailing to Byzantium" provides a comparable centripetal force as the resonating center of the poem's inner awareness. Both poems are mature in that the experience of change as a reality imposed on us has engraved itself on the phrasing and created the time-depths of the affective movement. Where "Memory" shoots straight into the emotional heart of the matter, "Sailing to Byzantium" dances up to the mark and then around and away from it. It holds more elements in balance, all controlled by the straightforward, idiomatic, and unhappy language of the protagonist in the opening lines of the first two stanzas that reemerges in the climax at the end of the third stanza.

I think it rather important that we reopen Yeats's poetry in this simple fashion. For one thing, it enables us to gauge the proper weight of the shorter lyrics. They are (as we saw earlier with the pivotal "The Road at My Door" and "The Stare's Nest by My Window" in "Meditations in Time of Civil War") touchstones of emotional authority and, often, keystones for a sequence or a volume. Moreover, they parallel the longer poems' crucial moments. It is not a matter of their being less "important." Obviously, an intellectually or symbolically elaborate surface does not in itself make for superior poetry (although many critics, I am convinced, do not find this point obvious at all but fancy that the ingenuity and laborious research necessary for their commentaries are the marks of a poet's significance). Obviously, too, we do a poet no honor by praising him for being something "more" than a poet—a philosopher or moralist or prophet, say. Nor do we reduce him by saying he is none of these things, or only inadequately so. Our key modern aesthetic equation is: *realization = resolution*. And *realization* is the kick of life, the quickened arousal of emotional consciousness that puts a complex of awareness in perspective. "Memory" is a tiny model of Yeats's mature work. It flings without hesitation into the climactic resolution that also completes its movement, transcending its "problem" by finding an image warm with life for the problem itself.

"Sailing to Byzantium" has a more conventional overt structure, placing its moment of illumination in the next-to-last stanza. But Yeats was also able to begin with such a moment of sharp illumination, as in the first half of "Leda and the Swan." The sexually charged dynamics of those lines acts out the god's assault on Leda and then her seduction and orgasmic response. The rest of the poem points away from this experiential center, but is essentially an improvisation that merely frames the drama and mystery of sexual possession. Yeats begins his sonnet with an attempt to imagine how it felt to be Leda taken suddenly by a doubly alien force: the swan ("brute blood of the air") that is really Zeus in disguise. The language of this male attempt to project female response is so voluptuously and humanly sexual, however, that it is clear the real effort of the poem is to realize how a woman experiences lovemaking, especially lovemaking that begins as rape. I am not talking about the poem's general "meaning"—its concluding question about human understanding and destiny in relation to the myth of Leda and perhaps of the Virgin Birth—but rather of the obsessive preoccupation of its language.

In thinking of Yeats's more complex poems, it is well to remember that they are spun around moments and passages of the kind I have been discussing. These moments and passages provide either the real resolutions of poems or the central preoccupations clarified by their supposed resolutions. The vision at the end of "Sailing to Byzantium," the rhetorical question at the end of "Leda and the Swan," only return us to the indissoluble, passionate centers of the poems.

I have been leading up to consideration of Yeats's mature lyric poetry generally. It can be reasonably argued that he reached his full poetic maturity with the poems in *The Tower* (1928), published when he was sixty-three—the same age as Pound was in 1948 when *The Pisan Cantos* appeared. But the poems of his two preceding volumes, *The Wild Swans at Coole* (1919) and *Michael Robartes and the Dancer* (1921), are well on the way to the level of *The Tower* and should be considered as part of the same powerful burst of poetic energy. As we have seen, the key sequences of the 1928 volume, "Meditations in Time of Civil War" and "Nineteen Hundred and Nineteen," were first published between 1919 and 1923.

The poems in these volumes that most clearly show the human base of his method, revealed in the passionate centers we have been discussing that are essential to his poetic purpose, are often dismissed or virtually ignored. "Memory" is an example in *The Wild Swans at Coole.* Two poems in *Michael Robartes and the Dancer* spring to mind: "An Image from a Past Life" and "Towards Break of Day." We might call them marriage-poems because they seem, without saying so, to involve husband and wife and were in fact written not very long after Yeats's own marriage in 1917. At any rate, they present a man and a woman intimately together, lovers committed to one another yet oppressed by the man's longing for his unpurged past. The title of "An Image from a Past Life" might just as well be "Memory" again, for the "image" referred to invades the speaker's present life just as in the shorter poem. It is characteristic that one critic simply dismisses what goes on in this poem. He grants that it is "exquisite" but objects that "it relies too much for its coherence on Yeats's complex note explaining the 'Over Shadower or Ideal Form.' "*

Now, Yeats's note is indeed charmingly complex and roundabout. Essentially it "explains" the image of a woman that, in this poem, intrudes on the couple and makes itself visible to the woman. Yeats's note says that the image is literally from a past life—that is, from an earlier incarnation—and he weaves some mystical con-

---

*Harold Bloom, *Yeats* (New York: Oxford University Press, 1970), p. 314. For Yeats's note, see *The Variorum Edition of the Poems of W. B. Yeats* (New York: Macmillan, 1957), pp. 821–23.

cepts into the explanation meanwhile. It is a sweetly heady note but hardly explains the poem, which as usual needs no explanation except its own nature. One might as well argue that a poem by Yeats referring, as this poem does, to "a sweetheart from another life" who comes to oppress his new love's psyche must of course refer to his famous old love, the beautiful Maud Gonne, and that his elaborate comment here is primarily intended to divert his wife's attention. Perhaps, but none of this is in the poem itself; nor does the poem rely on Yeats's ideas as given in the note.

To begin with, the poem is a dialogue, initiated by the man. He is the speaker in the first stanza, which consists of a series of four distinct utterances. The first is ambiguous, sudden, excited—very much like the opening line of Pound's Canto 47. The second is an eerie image of starlight reflected in a dark stream; it suggests brilliant, cold meanings that are humanly incomprehensible. The third is a parallel image, aural rather than visual this time, and more shocking in effect. The fourth characterizes the affect of the stanza; it expresses a conscious realization attending the experiences the speaker has just been describing. The "coherence" of the stanza lies in the relationship of these utterances, not in the afterthoughts that shaped Yeats's comment or in any biographical information we may have. The naked poem, its successive notes and tones and complex of intrinsic connections, must be read by its own light. Here is how it begins:

> He. Never until this night have I been stirred.
> The elaborate starlight throws a reflection
> On the dark stream,
> Till all the eddies gleam;
> And thereupon there comes that scream
> From terrified, invisible beast or bird:
> Image of poignant recollection.

The woman's reply picks up from the stanza's closing line. The music of her response is of a psychic shock beyond the man's. She has been possessed, while she slept, by an image out of *his* memory—not "poignant" for her but "bitter":

> *She.* An image of my heart that is smitten through
> Out of all likelihood, or reason,
> And when at last,
> Youth's bitterness being past,
> I had thought that all my days were cast
> Amid most lovely places, smitten as though
> It had not learned its lesson.

They have both been awakened by a disturbing, oddly shared dream or manifestation. But "She" is the one who actually *sees* the image in the air as they gaze out the window together. Further on she describes it: "A sweetheart from another life floats there / As though she had been forced to linger / From vague distress/ Or arrogant loveliness." The dialogue, then, counterposes contradictory sets of interlocking intensities. The stanzas, with their gracefully contracting and expanding line-pattern and their concentration of triple rhymes at the center of each, help reinforce the reciprocal, antiphonal music of this shared entrancement and dismay. Notes of male arrogance and guilt, together with female fear of domination, are present as well. The mixture of affects is comparable with that in the far more acutely painful "Towards Break of Day," another poem of dual dreams:

> Was it the double of my dream
> The woman that by me lay
> Dreamed, or did we halve a dream
> Under the first gleam of day?
>
> I thought: "There is a waterfall
> Upon Ben Bulben side

That all my childhood counted dear;
Were I to travel far and wide
I could not find a thing so dear."
My memories had magnified
So many times childhood delight.

I would have touched it like a child
But knew my finger could but have touched
Cold stone and water. I grew wild,
Even accusing Heaven because
It had set down among its laws:
Nothing that we love over-much
Is ponderable to our touch.

I dreamed towards break of day,
The cold blown spray in my nostril.
But she that beside me lay
Had watched in bitterer sleep
The marvellous stag of Arthur,
That lofty white stag, leap
From mountain steep to steep.

In this tale of twin despairs, the man's possession by a past at once renewed and irretrievable (the middle stanzas are a concretization of this paradox) goes far back into childhood. The memory of women's love is suggested, if at all, only tangentially in the general reference to what "we love over-much" and in the archetypal waterfall-image. The woman's dream is of a glamorous image of virile power, "the marvellous stag of Arthur," that eludes her touch. The poem begins with an abrupt, wonderstruck question that at the same time suggests a coolness between the pair. "The woman that by me lay" is hardly a warmly affectionate expression. Then, again abruptly, the tone and focus shift. Although the spotlight was on the woman at first, the second and third stanzas seem to forget her. Instead, the second stanza is all ecstatic memory of childhood feeling. In his dream,

the speaker has seen once more the waterfall he loved
when a boy—has seen it with a "delight" many times
increased in retrospect. This feeling modulates, in the
third stanza, into its opposite as a cold, depressive realism (familiar in Yeats) breaks into the dream. The new
mood was foreshadowed by the speaker's allusion in the
first stanza to "the first gleam of day" and by his observation in the second that his memories had "magnified"
his childhood delight. Now, in the third stanza, the
charmed waterfall of memory is suddenly diminished to
the image of "cold stone and water" standing between
him and his desired recovery of the touch of joy. The atmosphere is of "wild" frustration and, by implication in
this context, of sexual unhappiness. The language of
coldness and impersonality carries into the closing
stanza: "the cold blown spray in my nostril." Finally, we
have the even "bitterer" dream-experience of the
woman—her vision of an image of sexual neglect, for
which all this language of coldness and hardness and
wetness and the thwarting of the need to touch has
readied us.

Is her experience really more bitter than the man's?
He, we must remember, is the speaker. It is he who
presumes to report her feelings. What we have, then, is
in part a projection of his own guilt or humiliation.
Hence his opening question, seeking to connect the two
dreams. Once we see the reciprocity between the poem's
beginning and its ending, we must see the second stanza
in an altered light as well. The whole poem changes, as
though invisibly revised. The second stanza now has
something of the character of a wounded retreat from a
sexual impasse, into a childhood realm that turns disap-
pointingly into an embodiment of the speaker's adult
predicament. Meanwhile, *out there* in the world of women's dreams and perhaps in the lives of other men,

there is another kind of existence where freedom and joy prevail (seen in the elusive symbol of the stag the woman watches "leap / From mountain steep to steep"). The remarkably improvised form of this poem, incidentally, has the same surface suggestion of a simple pattern, and the same kind of complex variables in its inner structure, as does its emotional movement.

Again and again, an essential antithesis emerges in Yeats's poetry between the complexity of his speaker's whole consciousness and Yeats's own desire to strip the language down to the most direct expression possible of a private state of feeling. Romantic poetry began the modern movement toward this kind of antithesis. Contemporary poetry, when confessional, attempts to expose the poet in his or her psychic nakedness—a tendency that has infected much other poetry besides the overtly confessional. Yeats's work is well on the way toward this existential emphasis with its exhibitionist possibilities. It is true that in *The Tower* and even later he quite often employs a special romantic rhetoric and symbolistic scaffolding. His sequence "A Man Young and Old" (in *The Tower*), for instance, makes an inconsistent effort to relate the progress of his protagonist's love-experience symbolically to the phases of the moon. In "First Love," the protagonist opens the sequence by describing the woman he has loved as though she were the moon. She moves through her phases, beautiful and indifferent, humanly feminine in appearance but leaving darkness and turmoil behind her.

> She smiled and that transfigured me
> And left me but a lout,
> Maundering here, and maundering there,
> Emptier of thought
> Than the heavenly circuit of its stars
> When the moon sails out.

One can see how, in "First Love," Yeats attempts to assimilate the private and the cosmic to one another. The speaker views himself as the victim of his passion for a woman who is less a woman than she is a "sailing moon," the stonyhearted though glowing embodiment of impersonal cyclical process. But the most striking, and humanly the most stripped down, poem in "A Man Young and Old" is "The Death of the Hare." It is a peal of guilty recognition, close in feeling to the ending of "Towards Break of Day." In the midst of so many poems that mingle astronomical and other symbolism with a sort of modernized Petrarchan love-complaint, full of courtly sighs and flourishes and talk of "cruel happiness" in which "lovers drown," Yeats introduces a chilling thought about the real nature of courtship. The contrast is especially pointed between the earlier posture of lover as victim and the piercing insight here into the victimization of women in the love-hunt. Though the thought is not the same in the two poems, it is interesting that again, as in the unposturing image at the climax of "Memory," the woman is seen in the figure of a hare—

> I have pointed out the yelling pack,
> The hare leap to the wood,
> And when I pass a compliment
> Rejoice as lover should
> At the drooping of an eye,
> At the mantling of the blood.
>
> Then suddenly my heart is wrung
> By her distracted air
> And I remember wildness lost
> And after, swept from there,
> Am set down standing in the wood
> At the death of the hare.

Before looking any further into *The Tower*, I should like go back to *The Wild Swans at Coole* for a bit and to one poem there, "The Phases of the Moon," especially. This poem later became the poetic introduction to Yeats's *A Vision* (1925). It is generally treated as a verse exposition of the essential lunar symbolism of that prose work. Of course, it can be so read, but it is a lyric poem and only incidentally didactic. Indeed, *A Vision* itself is far more poetic in character and structure than one might think. I shall not pursue this fact beyond noting that it includes sixteen poems and poetic passages, half of them quoted from other poets, all of which touch in some way on the point of intersection between the supernatural and the mortal. The most strategically placed of these, in addition to "The Phases of the Moon," are two poems later published in *The Tower*. One is "Leda and the Swan" (called "Leda" in *A Vision*), which comes at the start of Book V, the portion that deals with the nature of historical epochs since 2000 B.C. The Other is "All Souls' Night: An Epilogue." That the poetry is an integral part of *A Vision* seems natural enough when one considers that a number of the prose passages read like this one:

> A civilisation is a struggle to keep self-control, and in this it is like some great tragic person, some Niobe who must display an almost superhuman will or the cry will not touch our sympathy. The loss of control over thought comes toward the end; first a sinking in upon the moral being, then the last surrender, the irrational cry, revelation—the scream of Juno's peacock.

What I want particularly to suggest here, however, is that "The Phases of the Moon" is not only a lyric poem but an exquisite one, with a highly confessional dimension of self-doubt. Its combined poignancy, humor,

ironic characterization, narrative and descriptive boldness, and range of emotional tones would seem to guarantee critical attention to its qualities as poetry. However, because it presents a dialogue in which some key
ideas of *A Vision* are expounded, its poetic achievement
has been neglected. The reason, quite simply, is its originality. Yeats created something new in this poem, using
the exposition for a glittering tonal display. An experiment in lyric structure, comparable despite its orderly
progression to, say, Canto 29 or Canto 81, it may be our
prime modern example of a work of poetic art that assimilates a developed exposition in this way. The poem's
movement converts the systematic thoughts into a series
of affects serving a completely different purpose than the
supposed clarification of a symbolic system. It is anything but a verse-crib for lazy students of *A Vision*, and
to describe it as "Yeats's most didactic poem"* is to
suggest a deadliness in a poem that is by turns mysterious, full of pure joy, brilliantly transporting, and crackling with exasperated self-irony.

A glance through the pages will suggest a good deal
about the straightforward yet complex structure of this
poem (the same deceptive combination, but on a larger
scale, as we have observed in such other poems as
"Memory" and "Towards Break of Day"). First, there is
an ultimate narrator, whose voice we hear in the italicized lines at the very beginning, shortly after the
middle, and at the end of the poem. He presents and
describes the two characters whose dialogue, printed as
in a play-script, is the main body of "The Phases of the
Moon." These characters, Aherne and Robartes, an older
and a younger man dressed like country folk, have

---

*Richard Ellmann, *The Identity of Yeats* (New York: Oxford University Press,
1954), pp. 158. To be fair, Ellmann does qualify this statement intelligently—
without, however, seeing the poem in its own right.

paused in their travels on a small bridge just outside a tower. High up in the tower, working by candlelight, sits the poet who has imagined them into being, and the reason they have paused here—on their way wherever they have come from to wherever they are going—is (unbeknownst to him) to mock his labors of imagination.

Why do they mock him? The poetic answer lies in the dance of opposed tonalities, and it includes hints of the poet's wry irony toward his own solitary labors. By way of Robartes, Yeats makes a facetious little joke about himself. Robartes explains that his own grievances date back to the time that Yeats wrote about both characters in prose works published in 1896 and 1897.*

> *Robartes.* He wrote of me in that extravagant style
> He had learnt from Pater, and to round his tale
> Said I was dead; and dead I choose to be.

Robartes is the main speaker in the poem, and Aherne is his admiring companion. It is "natural" for them to share this comic grudge, in their literary never-never land, against the author who not only described them in an outmoded style but then killed Robartes off as well. But as the poem unfolds, their mockery is felt also as the malign resistance of the unknown to being revealed. They are sure they know the secret of human fatality that the poet seeks. As mischievous sprites of a sort they are terribly sophisticated, and yet they have arrived only to gloat over him, to whisper over the great secret and think what fine tormenting tricks they might play on him.

More essentially, there is the unconscious mockery of their self-deception. They themselves, and their knowledge, are the poet's creation. " 'Mine author sung it

---

*See W. B. Yeats, *Mythologies* (New York: Macmillan, 1959)—especially "Rosa Alchemica," "The Tables of the Law," and "The Adoration of the Magi."

me,' " says Aherne, quoting some unspecified old text but indicating unconsciously where the knowledge comes from. This dimension of the poem is the painful one, the modern turn on romantic self-irony. The poet's own vision torments him. Because he knows the limits of his imagination, his best efforts become fruitless and grotesque in his own eyes. This pilgrimage of Robartes and Aherne is more consciously self-ironic than the one Eliot's protagonist makes in "Little Gidding."

Nevertheless, the vision is serious. In the main body of the poem, his two creations contemplate the poet in his tower and recite the great secret of "the changes of the moon" and the corresponding phases of any human life—all of them separate "cradles a man must needs be rocked in." When the revelatory recitation is finished the poet's vigil ends as well, his candle goes out, and the laughter of Aherne is heard as darkness takes over.

Within this general movement of the poem, the succession of affects comes on with as many shifts and startling juxtapositions as one finds in *The Cantos* at their most effective or in a sequence like "A Man Young and Old." The opening words of the narrator provide a homespun, realistic description that, at the same time, arouses expectation in the manner of any tale. The travelers have heard a sound and the older man has "cocked his ear." The dialogue begins with the natural question by Aherne: "What made that sound?" Robartes's reply immediately suggests the enormous range of associations, natural and mystical, involved in the poem:

> A rat or water-hen
> Splashed, or an otter slid into the stream.
> We are on the bridge; that shadow is the tower,
> And the light proves that he is reading still.
> He has found, after the manner of his kind,
> Mere images; chosen this place to live in

> Because, it may be, of the candle-light
> From the far tower where Milton's Platonist
> Sat late, or Shelley's visionary prince:
> The lonely light that Samuel Palmer engraved,
> An image of mysterious wisdom won by toil;
> And now he seeks in book or manuscript
> What he shall never find.

These words do not dispel the folk-tale atmosphere of the beginning, but they surely superimpose a sophisticated speaking intelligence. We have encountered "Milton's Platonist" (from "Il Penseroso") before, in discussing "Meditations in Time of Civil War." Shelley's "Prince Athanase: A Fragment" shows us the "visionary prince" Robartes refers to, who dwelt "apart from men, as in a lonely tower." Samuel Palmer's engraving, "The Lonely Tower," first appeared in an edition of Milton as an illustration for "Il Penseroso." All these allusions prepare us for the intellectual and imaginative heights of Robartes's later speeches—despite his appearance, he is no uneducated countryman. They also serve to characterize the poet in the tower as one who, like Milton and Shelley, seeks "an image of mysterious wisdom won by toil." Down below, as real as ever, is the busy animal life of earth and stream, going on in the shadow of the tower. There too stand the bearers of the "mysterious wisdom" the poet seeks. "Mere images" themselves after all, they talk of him with facetious malice.

The beginning, then, opens the way for the coupling of realism and fantasy, humor and grave intensity, in the language that follows. And yet, once the central incantatory music of the poem gets under way, its delphic character and concentrated invocation of visionary imagery are in an entirely different key from what has gone before.

> *Aherne.* Sing me the changes of the moon once more;
> True song, though speech: "mine author sung it me."

Robartes. Twenty-and-eight the phases of the moon,
   The full and the moon's dark and all the crescents,
   Twenty-and-eight, and yet but six-and-twenty
   The cradles that a man must needs be rocked in:
   For there's no human life at the full or the dark.
   From the first crescent to the half, the dream
   But summons to adventure and the man
   Is always happy like a bird or a beast . . .

Starting with this speech, Robartes "sings" his knowledge in some sixty lines or more of direct exposition, interrupted by questions and comments from Aherne and some incidental exchanges of thought with him. The gist of the moon-symbolism is that the course of a human life corresponds to that of the moon passing through its phases from dark to full and back to dark again. In the first half of one's life the active, creative, subjective self is in the ascendancy and one "follows whatever whim's most difficult / Among whims not impossible." The self seems to dominate the objective world more and more, and at the full of its development so imposes its will on reality that it cannot distinguish its own identity from everything outside it. The process is reversed in the second half of life; one becomes more and more the creature of objective forces until distorted out of all recognition and at last obliterated. A further implication is that cultures pass through the same phases, and that each phase has its characteristic dominant personalities and divinities. This scheme of the cycles of fatality is essentially familiar and simple, with innumerable antecedents in literature and lore. It is either rational or superstitious, depending on where one's emphasis falls, and Yeats plays these opposites against one another to make a poem full of both magical imagination and grim pessimism.

The point I wish to emphasize is this last one, the po-

etic use of the scheme. It enables Yeats (by way of Robartes, who is clearly an alternative self) to isolate and
yet relate pure will and pure fatality, in a series of remarkable leaps of vision. He is especially inspired in his
images of the ideal beauty and heroism which, once realized, must lose force and focus:

> But while the moon is rounding towards the full
> He follows whatever whim's most difficult
> Among whims not impossible, and though scarred,
> As with the cat-o'-nine tails of the mind,
> His body moulded from within his body
> Grows comelier. Eleven pass, and then
> Athene takes Achilles by the hair,
> Hector is in the dust, Nietzsche is born,
> Because the hero's crescent is the twelfth.
> And yet, twice born, twice buried, grow he must,
> Before the full moon, helpless as a worm . . .
> The soul begins to tremble into stillness,
> To die into the labyrinth of itself!

At this point, as it were, the poem outgrows both the
poet in his tower, dreaming his way into the system,
and the singer who "knows" it already. The system is for
the moment forgotten as Robartes and Aherne fall into
an entranced dialogue on what happens when we actually stamp our wills on reality and the soul "dies into the
labyrinth of itself." The dialogue is a triumph of post-
Romantic poetic imagination. It reaches past the tragic
view to assert the permanence of transcendent states.
They do not vanish. They are not "mere" dreams that
the touch of reality destroys or proves poisonous. Nor do
they show joy as possible merely in fleeting moments of
elusive grace—Eliot's notion in "Burnt Norton" that
"human kind / Cannot bear very much reality" of the
Platonic or revelatory variety.

Yeats, rather, pursues the psychological "truth" here

that what we become and what we create do endure, in a
realm at least tangential to that of ordinary mortality.
This "truth," which underlies artistic effort and human
morale generally, is a passionate insistence of the poem.
In the dialogue I have just mentioned, the somewhat
earthier Aherne gives a sexual turn to Robartes's images
of the lengthening reach of desire. The intimate in-
wardness of his thought paradoxically catapults Robartes's vision outside the pattern he has been expounding.
Now the poem reaches its heights of feeling. Its language
of combined subjective insinuation and Romantic
strangeness balances exuberance and terror:

Aherne.   All dreams of the soul
  End in a beautiful man's or woman's body.

Robartes. Have you not always known it?
Aherne.   The song will have it
  That those who have loved got their long fingers
  From death, and wounds, or on Sinai's top,
  Or from some bloody whip in their own hands.
  They ran from cradle to cradle till at last
  Their beauty dropped out of the loneliness
  Of body and soul.

Robartes.   The lover's heart knows that.

Aherne. It must be that the terror in their eyes
  Is memory or foreknowledge of the hour
  When all is fed with light and heaven is bare.

Robartes. When the moon's full those creatures of the full
  Are met on the waste hills by countrymen
  Who shudder and hurry by: body and soul
  Estranged amid the strangeness of themselves,
  Caught up in contemplation, the mind's eye
  Fixed upon images that once were thought;
  For separate, perfect, and immovable
  Images can break the solitude
  Of lovely, satisfied, indifferent eyes.

It would be easy to dismiss all this imagery of perfect fulfilment, perfect detachment, as marvelous spooky nonsense (and perhaps, in an absolute fever of dismissal, even omit the word "marvelous"). But we have in this passage an instance of rhapsodic letting-go rare in modern poetry. Not that the diction of pain and solitude permits a sense of *delight* as we ordinarily understand it, but Yeats has seized on the access of self-contained ecstasy in the aftermath of creative action and has held on to his vision of it. He has not been frightened off by the bitter dimensions of the experience. Although Robartes goes on to detail the soul's return to darkness in the second half of life, this held vision controls the emotional life of the poem. In the second half everything human and commanding becomes deformed and servile, submitting to nature's tendency to break down the beautiful forms that the life-force and the human will have nourished. And yet, in the stanza that describes the characteristic human masks of deformity in the last crescent—"Hunchback and Saint and Fool": embodiments respectively of physical distortion, devout submission to whatever fate holds, and intellectual emptiness—something of the contemplative rapture of full awareness remains to leaven the poem's spirit:

Robartes. Hunchback and Saint and Fool are the last crescents.
  The burning bow that once could shoot an arrow
  Out of the up and down, the wagon-wheel
  Of beauty's cruelty and wisdom's chatter—
  Out of that raving tide—is drawn betwixt
  Deformity of body and of mind.

In important ways, the fanciful "The Phases of the Moon" prefigures the more vigorously personal and volatile poetry of *The Tower*. It is a model of lyrical control over unwieldy elements, and of placing divergent modes of imagination in tandem so that they seem naturally continuous. So placed, for example, the moments of visionary transport, the derisory speeches and laughter, and the darker notes of fatality toward the end take on a complex reciprocity characteristic of heightened sensibility in our era. The sense of moving out of the deep strengths of traditional beliefs and symbolic assumptions into a chaos of possibility is always with us, and is reflected even in the passage just quoted. The arbitrary juxtaposition of modes of feeling seems a necessary condition of this state.

This is not really an intellectual matter. The beliefs and struggles of past culture are the very stuff of subjective reality. Our instinctive premise that the key to transcendence lies in intensity of awareness is linked to the presence in us of that subjective float of the living past. Objectively and analytically, meanwhile, we tend simply to ignore or reject that latent presence or to subject it to acid scrutiny. The opposed skepticism and entrancement of "The Phases of the Moon" mark out this battle-arena of spirit. The moments of rhapsodic letting-go act out a kind of hope beyond hope, or insistence beyond despair, a release of visionary energy that involves the same risk as the one accepted by Pound-Odysseus in Canto 47.

The new stress on the image in modern poetry has something to do with its combined objective and subjective character. Much earlier than "The Phases of the Moon," Yeats had recognized the potency of "abstract," "impersonal" images—the enormous emotional energy locked into them and also their power, by transference or displacement, to liberate personal expression. An example is "He Hears the Cry of the Sedge," which when first published in 1897 read:

> I wander by the edge
> Of this desolate lake,
> Where wind cries in the sedge,
> *Until the axle break*
> *That keeps the stars in their round,*
> *And hands hurl in the deep*
> *The banners of East and West,*
> *And the girdle of light is unbound,*
> *Your breast will not lie on the breast*
> *Of your beloved in sleep.*

The "axle that keeps the stars in their round," "the deep," and "the girdle of light" are cosmological abstractions that by implication are fraught with Biblical, astrological, and analogous associations. The lonely Keatsian speaker touches all potential human turmoil ("the banners of East and West," in fact) when these images enter his mind. In turn, that turmoil invades the erotic pathos of the two closing lines.

Even more effective and interesting is the dynamic shift at the end of "Adam's Curse," written some five years later. In this delicate yet sometimes vehement poem, Yeats introduces himself and two women in deep conversation—

> We sat together at one summer's end,
> That beautiful mild woman, your close friend,
> And you and I, and talked of poetry.

The "you" does not speak, but the other two lose themselves in a discussion of values gone out of phase. Those who now set the world's standards think poets are nothing but idlers; the cultivation of womanly grace and beauty is a labor equally unappreciated by the world—"they do not talk of it at school"; and the ancient courtly conception of a lover has certainly grown obsolete. Then

the impersonal cosmic image enters the poem, with all
its ancient symbolism, and opens the way for the intimately personal ending addressed to the silent "you":

> We sat grown quiet at the name of love;
> We saw the last embers of daylight die,
> And in the trembling blue-green of the sky
> A moon, worn as if it had been a shell
> Washed by time's waters as they rose and fell
> About the stars and broke in days and years.
>
> I had a thought for no one's but your ears:
> That you were beautiful, and that I strove
> To love you in the old high way of love;
> That it had all seemed happy, and yet we'd grown
> As weary-hearted as that hollow moon.

These lovely earlier pieces and others like them confirmed a method that perhaps reached its perfection,
within a relatively simple structure, in "Easter 1916." In
that poem Yeats interrupts his contemplation of the
tragically ennobling effects of the Easter Rebellion on its
executed leaders with another impersonal image. It is
not cosmic this time—no stars or moon or constella-
tions—but a metaphor of shared political purpose which
grows directly out of the questions about the Rebellion
that have been puzzling him despite his affectionate celebration of its martyrs:

> Hearts with one purpose alone
> Through summer and winter seem
> Enchanted to a stone
> To trouble the living stream.
> The horse that comes from the road,
> The rider, the birds that range
> From cloud to tumbling cloud,
> Minute by minute they change;
> A shadow of cloud on the stream

> Changes minute by minute;
> A horse-hoof slides on the brim,
> And a horse plashes within it;
> The long-legged moor-hens dive,
> And hens to moor-cocks call;
> Minute by minute they live:
> The stone's in the midst of all.

The stone-image puts the political direction of the poem in a new light. Hardness is not always a value in human thought and feeling, not when it precludes sensitivity to reality and openness to change. The intrusion of the stanza of nature-imagery—hard stone, flowing stream, endless variety and change—brings in a world of reference entirely alien to political determinism. "Hearts with one purpose alone . . . enchanted to a stone" began as an admiring image for steadfast idealism. But when the full set of associations has made itself felt, the very same image has swung the poem elsewhere, and the closing stanza begins:

> Too long a sacrifice
> Can make a stone of the heart.

The speaker has been freed to release all the thoughts that political dogmatism represses. In the final lines the cherished martyrs are still cherished, but they are no longer heroes in the full meaning of the word. Rather, they were "bewildered" by "excess of love." The stone-image has enabled the speaker to become a free man in realizing his true feeling, and the earlier celebration becomes richer and more humanly manysided as a result.

The naturalness, pliancy, and volatility of Yeats's phrasing in "Easter 1916" are aspects of his poetic maturing that can be matched in a number of other poems in *The Wild Swans at Coole* and *Michael Robartes and the Dancer* (the first book in which it appeared, although it was privately printed in pamphlet form in 1916). What "The Phases of the Moon" embodied, apart from a developing interest in more complex structures that would be manifested in later sequences, was the ripening of various other qualities as well that one must identify as aspects of poetic *character*—for instance, robust humor, dramatic boldness, uninhibited imaginative leaps, and the courage of self-ridicule. With these qualities comes an ease in handling their nuances: quietly gentle modes of humor, touches of characterization or dramatic suggestiveness, moments of exaltation held for a few brief lines only, perhaps, and very often wryly qualified in some way, and a candor that exposes the speaker's unheroic nature.

The infinitely engaging "Demon and Beast," in *Michael Robartes and the Dancer*, is a case in point. It presents and considers a feeling of sudden joy and freedom that overcame the speaker for a short time—"for certain minutes at the least"—and released him from his usual state of being plagued by rival forces pulling him back and forth: the "demon" of his intellectual passions, the "beast" of bodily desire. For those minutes, too, he could put the oppression of Irish history and of his sense of coming death away; he moved among portraits in Dublin's Municipal Gallery that would ordinarily seem foreboding, and all seemed to smile. Even a death's head in one of the paintings "said / Welcome." Then, in Stephen's Green nearby, he watched birds, a gull and "an absurd / Portly green-pated bird," and was aroused to tears: "Being no more demoniac / A stupid happy creature / Could rouse my whole nature." He explains that it was merely growing old, which brings "chilled blood," that filled him with this feeling of sweetness that he would like to have go on indefinitely. The poem ends with an exuberant allusion to St. Anthony and his ascetic monastic community who starved themselves joyously to death in the fourth century. It is as though some old gentleman had fixed us with his glittering eye and begun, apparently, to maunder on about his health and about various things he has read and thought, and we realized as he talked that a brilliant, confiding spirit was conveying his dearest and inmost feelings to us, with a network of implications as involved as that in "The Phases of the Moon."

When we pitch into *The Tower* we find a proliferation of energies and a heightening of vigorous, concrete concentration along the lines we have been discussing. The beginning of the title-poem shows the poet taking center stage and exhibiting his weakness and misery with a sort of zest—

> What shall I do with this absurdity—
> O heart, O troubled heart—this caricature,
> Decrepit age that has been tied to me
> As to a dog's tail?

He has made a comic figure of himself, in that grotesque sense in which it becomes hard to sort out clowning from anguish. Imagine a figure with a mask of old age hobbling out before an audience, reciting these lines, and then leaving. Are they hilarious, heartbreaking, or both? They violate a certain social assumption: that human dignity requires that we not complain about a necessary human predicament to which all people are subject. And yet they express an existential suffering.

But the poem does not end here. These lines are merely the opening of a wide-ranging three-part poem, one in which only the first part is a complaint against old age. The rest of the first part turns bitterly away from the violent, unanswerable question of the start and speaks

with a quiet, more philosophical despair. It even falls
into a Wordsworthian rhythm and phrasing for a few
lines as an ironic self-corrective. Yet at the end of the
passage we can see that the speaker is even more appalled than he seemed at first, for the issue is not simply
growing old but forgoing the passion of the artist in
order to take on a role more suitable at his age lest he appear humiliatingly pathetic:

> Never had I more
> Excited, passionate, fantastical
> Imagination, nor an ear and eye
> That more expected the impossible—
> No, not in boyhood when with rod and fly,
> Or the humbler worm, I climbed Ben Bulben's back
> And had the livelong summer day to spend.
> It seems that I must bid the Muse go pack,
> Choose Plato and Plotinus for a friend
> Until imagination, ear and eye,
> Can be content with argument and deal
> In abstract things; or be derided by
> A sort of battered kettle at the heel.

If the speaker is dismayed at what is expected of him,
it should be clear that he has no intention of complying.
What he says about himself is an assertion of mobilized
power. "Battered kettle at the heel" or not, he will accept
the humiliation of a decrepit body and live with the
Muse as before. And so, in the witty, reminiscent, anec-
dotal, and finally "excited, passionate, fantastical" second part, he summons up many figures out of local tradition, and one figure of his own creation—Red Hanrahan,
"old lecher with a love on every wind"—to ask them all
the obvious question: *Have all the dead raged against old
age as I do?* The answer is too obvious to linger over, and
so he dismisses the impatient ghosts and asks
Hanrahan—like Robartes an alternative persona—still

another question, which must remain unanswered except by himself:

> Does the imagination dwell the most
> Upon a woman won or a woman lost?
> If on the lost, admit you turned aside
> From a great labyrinth out of pride,
> Cowardice, some silly over-subtle thought
> Or anything called conscience once;
> And that if memory recur, the sun's
> Under eclipse and the day blotted out.

Here is another obvious question. The indissoluble emotional centers of the poems are all just as obvious. Compare, for instance, the moments of sweet, free joy in "Demon and Beast," or the final view in "The Phases of the Moon" of demonic darkness as the light goes out in the tower and Aherne's laughter rings out. We have moved through several such emotional centers in "The Tower" so far. First there was the protagonist's anguished outcry at the start. Then came his wild invocation of all local ghosts and of past creations of his own fantasy, to find out whether others had ever accepted old age with more grace than he. This is the natural casting about of people in crisis for reassurance, but Part II blazes with near-comic intensity like that in the first lines. And now he has turned his mind to the intolerable pain of a recurrent memory, of his failure to accept a great love when it offered itself. All the thought and the digression woven around these moments are used to set them in precise context and to suggest the whole emotional diapason of their realization. Part II has demonstrated the speaker's thoroughly aroused, transforming imagination by conjuring up figures embodying the passionate life and mind. The imagination's supreme effort is to change fatality itself, by sheer force of a desire that is ultimately sexual:

> the tragedy began
> With Homer that was a blind man,
> And Helen has all living hearts betrayed.
> O may the moon and sunlight seem
> One inextricable beam,
> For if I triumph I must make men mad.

At the end of Part II, as we have seen, he has not triumphed. He is left with the tormenting memory of "woman lost." He has missed the dearest empathy of love by not losing himself in the "labyrinth" of her nature. But Part III takes a different tack. "It is time," he half-puns in the opening line, "that I wrote my will." Invoking an ideal human pride superior to ordinary ambitions and to the servility of politics, he proclaims the primacy of man's will over reason and fate. Although the tone is different—deliberately defiant and "mad"—his vision is similar to that of the entranced beings who escape the lunar system in "The Phases of the Moon." The tonal difference lies in the hard, assertive intensity here, for the whole effort is saturated with the counter-feeling of having met defeat. It is a brilliantly instructive section of the poem. It illustrates the conversion, in process, of motifs inert in themselves into independent affective energy. "Thought" here is awareness in action. To say that the poem is "about" Irish aristocratic pride, or about refusal to accept old age and thwarted love, or about will and fatality would only suggest points of reference shared with thousands of other poems and millions of prose statements. The motifs are only the flint from which the sparks of the poem are struck. The language in lines like "The people of Burke and Grattan / That gave, though free to refuse" is not to be discounted, but when the climactic passage takes off from these lines they recede very quickly:

> Pride, like that of the morn,
> When the headlong light is loose,
> Or that of the fabulous horn,
> Or that of the sudden shower
> When all streams are dry,
> Or that of the hour
> When the swan must fix his eye
> Upon a fading gleam,
> Float out upon a long
> Last reach of glittering stream
> And there sing his last song.
> And I declare my faith:
> I mock Plotinus' thought
> And cry in Plato's teeth,
> Death and life were not
> Till man made up the whole . . .

The defiant note carries bravely into the beginning of the final stanza: "Now shall I make my soul." But mainly the ending is given to images of loss and death. It is still assertive. In making himself a soul, the speaker says, he will learn to see his own bodily decay and the deaths of people he loves in a new way. They will seem insignificant—nothing more than "the clouds of the sky / When the horizon fades, / Or a bird's sleepy cry / Among the deepening shades." This concluding note is more touching than convincing, for it has been preceded by a devastating list of losses that amounts to the essence of human grief:

> the wreck of body,
> Slow decay of blood,
> Testy delirium
> Or dull decrepitude,
> Or what worse evil come—
> The death of friends, or death
> Of every brilliant eye
> That made a catch in the breath.

We are back—Yeats's poems keep returning to centers
of literal human feeling—to the essential predicament
that the poems of *The Tower* continuously focus on and
struggle against. The first poem, "Sailing to Byzantium,"
is a compressed dramatization of this predicament, un-
derscored by its climactic prayer to the speaker's supernatural mirror-images in the aestheticized heaven of a
Byzantine mosaic. The title-poem then, as we have seen,
expands both the view of the speaker's sufferings and
his dream of transcending the laws of natural change.
The speaker in "The Tower" assumes the task of transcendence himself rather than praying to the "sages
standing in God's holy fire" to transform him. He does
not care that his great speech on the power of man's will
to create whatever it desires will be thought irrational;
he has already proclaimed: "If I triumph I must make
men mad." These two poems present an uncompromis-
ing view of personal suffering and an equally un-
compromising vision of a state of ecstasy to be built by
the unyielding human soul. The volume as a whole
moves from dramatizing these fierce oppositions
(reoriented in partly political terms in the two sequences
that follow, which, however, stress the soul's solitude
rather than its triumph) to internalizing them in the closing poem, "All Souls' Night."

I do not mean to trace the whole movement of *The
Tower* now, but only to observe that it does move in relation to the emotional axes I have been noting. Two
poems stand at the center of its world of feeling, "Leda
and the Swan" and "Among School Children." The
former envisages apocalyptic change in terms of a sexual
act in which the human participant is seized, aroused,
and used—that is, impregnated with the seed of the future. The real affect of the poem, I have suggested, lies in

its curiosity about female sexuality (a point that might be made, with even more cautious qualification, about the middle section of "The Tower"). The male creative power that makes history, mythical as well as empirical, appears as a swan that is by no means the "solitary soul" it symbolizes in other poems—and yet, if Leda is the symbol of ordinary mortality, the fertile stuff of existence that is used as destiny wills, perhaps some ingenious psychoanalytical theorist can draw a valid conclusion or two about the drift of Yeats's fantasy. For us, looking at the work poetically, it is possible only to say that impersonal cosmos and individual human being are alike shown as driven by sexual energies implicit in all process, and that in "Leda and the Swan" the private sensibility that speaks elsewhere almost disappears from sight. At most he is the narrator, re-creating in excited imagination Leda's response to the god. And he is the philosopher of history. But the suffering man is invisible.

He is, though, extremely visible in "Among School Children," in which again he faces into a world of hidden female meanings. The school children are all girls, their teachers are nuns, and as he moves among them he is seized with the thought of how the woman he has loved must have looked and felt as a child, and of how it was to be with her at the height of her young womanhood, and of what she is like now that both of them are older. In this poem, however, all these realizations bear directly on the twin predicaments of old age and of the disparity between reality and the ideal. At the end of the poem the speaker insists that in process itself, in unconscious natural growth or in the creative act, we do transcend that disparity. Within this clearly developed frame of thought the phrasing moves from one climax of feel-

ing to the next, in surges of empathy with the children,
with his remembered love, and with the nuns, but most
of all with mothers in labor—

> What youthful mother, a shape upon her lap
> Honey of generation had betrayed,
> And that must sleep, shriek, struggle to escape
> As recollection or the drug decide,
> Would think her son, did she but see that shape
> With sixty or more winters on its head,
> A compensation for the pang of his birth,
> Or the uncertainty of his setting forth?

"All Souls' Night" draws all threads of the volume
together; it may be the most original and moving poem
of all. In it Yeats plays the role of a man so totally with-
drawn into his inner world of memory, and so familiar
with the expectation of death, that only the dead can be
his true companions. Only they will accept, without
laughter or tears, the "marvellous thing" he has to tell.
And even they must be drunk to do so. Again, as in
"The Tower" but more subtly here, the deeply serious
and the ludicrous are all but indistinguishable, and the
poet means it to be so. Then, as in the second part of
"The Tower," he summons up the dead—three old
friends this time—not to ask them rhetorical questions
but to have their intimate companionship while he masters by meditation the realm in which they exist. Perhaps he will pass over into it while not even aware of the
transition. The ritual wine, whimsically served, is to
bring the companions together; the occasion, of course,
is just right:

> Midnight has come, and the great Christ Church Bell
> And many a lesser bell sound through the room;
> And it is All Souls' Night,
> And two long glasses brimmed with muscatel

Bubble upon the table. A ghost may come;
For it is a ghost's right,
His element is so fine
Being sharpened by his death,
To drink from the wine-breath
While our gross palates drink from the whole wine.

Yeats's dead friends were also, as the poem tells us, students of mysticism and the occult. Each was by nature an intense person, and each had reason to be in an especially exacerbated state: one because of the death of his ardently cherished wife, another because a disfiguring disease had led her to leave home and teach in a far-off place "among dark skins," a third because his difficult, solitary life had made him "half a lunatic." Each was a "ghost-lover" who would have been as much at home as Yeats with the intricacies of *A Vision*. The poem takes pains to acquaint us with these affinities. The relationship shown between the first friend and his dead wife mirrors the strange, half-tragic exaltation of the poem.

Two thoughts were so mixed up I could not tell
Whether of her or God he thought the most,
But think that his mind's eye,
When upward turned, on one sole image fell;
And that a slight companionable ghost,
Wild with divinity,
Had so lit up the whole
Immense miraculous house
The Bible promised us,
It seemed a gold-fish swimming in a bowl.

The poignancy of each of the three lives is developed with tender sympathy, leavened here by a special delight touched with humor and elsewhere, in the case of the third friend, by an acerbic yet still kindly wit. Somehow they each have something of the speaker's own nature; and as ghosts they have a fineness of awareness superior to their specific former identities:

> But names are nothing. No matter who it be,
> So that his elements have grown so fine
> The fume of muscatel
> Can give his sharpened palate ecstasy
> No living man can drink from the whole wine.

The speaker has called upon kindred sensibilities among his dead acquaintances, yet fundamentally he is after the companionship of *pure* sensibility beyond his own. Such companionship would enable him to move back and forth between the two worlds like Eliot's "familiar compound ghost" (a phrase perhaps teased into being by the "slight companionable ghost" of this poem) in "Little Gidding." He could then go beyond the poor mocked poet of "The Phases of the Moon" and actually see the supernatural world on the other side of death.

> Such thought—such thought have I that hold it tight
> Till meditation master all its parts,
> Nothing can stay my glance
> Until that glance run in the world's despite
> To where the damned have howled away their hearts,
> And where the blessed dance;
> Such thought, that in it bound
> I need no other thing,
> Wound in mind's wandering
> As mummies in the mummy-cloth are wound.

The triumph in these closing lines is sharply qualified by the pathos of the speaker's situation. He is marshaling his resources for death and, as a first step, summoning dead friends to commune with. Moreover, terror as well as bliss attends his exalted reverie. Beyond this complex literal situation of the poem, however, the language reaches another plane: a state of ultimate readiness—that "ecstasy of pure sensibility" I have mentioned. The poem has been inducing this state of perfectly open volatility from the start, and each of the three dead friends is so described as to add to our increasing sense of it.

Here, I would argue, is the chief end of lyric poetry— to reach an equilibrium among the volatile possibilities that emerge in a poem. Tonalities stream around and away from a poem's emotional centers. They need the centers as base; otherwise their genuineness remains in question. Yet they take on independent force and, finally, the movement of feeling in a poem is all. In poetry sufficiently alive and accomplished, it culminates in a highly charged state of accumulated awareness such as we have seen gathering in "All Souls' Night."

Yeats is a modern poet by virtue of his mastery of this process. His confessional immediacy enabled him to exploit the raw energy of direct experience and uncensored feeling in poems whose surface seems, often, traditionally meditative. Violent historical change and the assault on sensibility of revolutionary changes in thought helped form a Yeatsian poetic of dynamic ambiguity combined with sharp clarity and frankness of crucial emotional statement. For my purposes here I have confined my discussion almost entirely to the poetry of *The Tower* and just before, the body of work containing the fruits of his slow, progressive maturing. In doing so, I have not meant to discount his work of the next decade, virtually up to his death early in 1939. Some of his most superb poetry was yet to come, including a whole series of sequences such as *Words for Music Perhaps, A Woman Young and Old*, the little group of poems led off by "The Three Bushes" in *New Poems,* and the original grouping of *Last Poems* that has not yet been printed properly in a collected volume.*

From the many things I should like to say (but shall not) about these later poems, I shall choose but a few, avoiding the temptation to discuss some very beautiful work in detail. I shall even avoid quoting lines that have sung in my ears for decades. One point to make certainly, however, is the proliferation of short, powerful poems with affects comparable to that of "Memory." Among these are "Death" (a compressed afterbeat of "The Tower"), the highly confessional "Remorse for Intemperate Speech" (in its forthright wretchedness perhaps the most telling of Yeats's political poems apart from those in "Meditations" and "Nineteen Hundred and Nineteen"), "Parnell," and "Politics." The sequences I have named, too, include a great many more such poems; Yeats remains our greatest modern architect of structures made up of lightning flashes. "The Three Bushes" and the six poems following it are a striking experiment in such a structure.

I would suggest, too, that a higher proportion of poems after *The Tower* than before are presentative, rather than discursive, in external form. If one compares "Byzantium" (in *The Winding Stair*, 1933) with "Sailing to Byzantium," for instance, one sees at once that it presents, without comment, a series of complex image-clusters. These image-clusters parallel one another and accumulate a steadily increasing pressure of realization. "Byzantium" reorients the earlier poem with a far greater sureness of climactic movement, and leaves critics with no handle for pedantic quarreling about its

---

* These sequences and others will be discussed in detail in a study of the modern poetic sequence I am preparing with Sally M. Gall. On the order of *Last Poems*, see Curtis Bradford, "Yeats's *Last Poems* Again," in *Yeats Centenary Papers*, edited by Liam Miller (Dublin: Dolmen Press, 1966), pp. 259–88.

thought. Poems like "Long-Legged Fly," "John Kinsella's Lament for Mrs. Mary Moore," "The Statesman's Holiday" (a wonderful instance of a musical burst of release from the limits of the traditional ode), "News for the Delphic Oracle," and "The Man and the Echo" are other examples. Even a tiny poem like the couplet "Parnell" is a veritable projectile of political passion—and the later political poems, whether written as "marching songs" or as personal statements, tend in general toward this condition of being vehement, essentially antipolitical explosions of feeling.

Yeats was a dramatist as well as a poet—a separate subject I dare not treat here because it would destroy the proportions of this book entirely. His plays need to be seen as poetry literally projected on the stage. Late in his life he wrote: "Browning said that he could not write a successful play because interested not in character in action but in action in character. I had begun to get rid of everything that is not, whether in lyric or dramatic poetry, in some sense character in action; a pause in the midst of action perhaps, but action always its end and theme."* Given the genius of his art and his peculiar combination of responsiveness and resistance to the self-destructive throes of a civilization, it was inevitable that his work should have informed several generations of poets after him. It has done so without fanfare of schools and movements, simply by the authority of its example.

* "An Introduction for My Plays," in *Essays and Introductions* (London: Macmillan, 1961), p. 530.

Chapter 7

Eliot:
ESSENCES AND OPEN FORMS

Eliot—the least prolific of poets, certainly of great poets who live to so ripe an age—was first precocious and then matured and exhausted his lyric talent sooner than most. In his early thirties he wrote the poem acclaimed as his masterpiece: "The Waste Land." His effective poetic career ended at the precise moment in 1942 when, at the age of fifty-four, he completed "Little Gidding."

One can sum up the career fairly quickly. His first book, *Prufrock and Other Observations* (1917) contained a dozen poems. It was reprinted, with a dozen more poems, in *Ara Vos Prec* (1920). Essentially the same book, with one substitution, was published under the title *Poems* in the United States in the same year. (Eliot's earlier books had appeared only in England.)* "The Waste Land" (1922), "The Hollow Men" (first published as a whole in 1925), the four "Ariel" poems (published sepa-

*I should notice a third British title—*Poems,* a pamphlet published in 1919. It contained six of the new poems later printed in *Ara Vos Prec.*

rately in 1927–30), "Ash Wednesday" (written 1927 and, like "The Hollow Men," published piecemeal before appearing as a whole), the two poems of *Coriolan* (published separately 1931–32), the two "Fragments" in *Sweeney Agonistes* (1932), and *Four Quartets* (first published separately in 1936, 1940, 1941, and 1942) make up the rest of his work that has any serious interest. Most of these titles are of relatively short sequences.

I have made a point of noting how many of the poems were published a section at a time as they struggled into final sequential form. "Ash Wednesday," for example, did not emerge as a six-part work until 1930. Part II was published in 1927, Part I in 1928, and Part III in 1929, all as separate poems with different names. Eliot composed in small units, working out of involved states of feeling often associated, in the poems themselves, with inhibition, fastidiousness, and an acute sense of the ridiculous. This last quality has little in common with the way Yeats sometimes made himself a figure of humiliation and ridicule. It is in the grain of Eliot's essential poetic sensibility, although he loosens up a good deal—for him—after 1925. His power of evocation is extraordinary and closely linked to something like social embarrassment in his early work. "The Love Song of J. Alfred Prufrock," his first published poem except in school and university magazines, is a perfect instance. It is the essential music of self-consciousness.

From the beginning his work shows powers of distilled intensity. To be any good at all it had to be more highly disciplined than that of almost anyone else, for everything depended so on precise technique—to get image, tone, idiom exactly right, one effect at a time, and so build into a total atmosphere saturating the entire work. Much of Yeats's early work and, even more, Pound's is engagingly bad, the work of a talented young man of uncertain promise mucking about with other people's outmoded language. Not so with Eliot. His early writing, seen in *Prufrock and Other Observations*, is self-consciously ironic and inward. It reflects a mind responsive to such models as Robert Browning and Jules Laforgue but already teaching itself to use them in its own way. It is a mind close in temper to the American generation of Henry Adams, Trumbull Stickney, and E. A. Robinson, with "Jamesian" fineness of discrimination—not exactly robust but not squeamish either. Everything Eliot does is experimental in some genuine sense.

Take the prose-poem "Hysteria" in the *Prufrock* group:

> As she laughed I was aware of becoming involved in her laughter and being part of it, until her teeth were only accidental stars with a talent for squad-drill. I was drawn in by short gasps, inhaled at each momentary recovery, lost finally in the dark caverns of her throat, bruised by the ripple. of unseen muscles. An elderly waiter with trembling hands was hurriedly spreading a pink and white checked cloth over the rusty green iron table, saying: "If the lady and gentleman wish to take their tea in the garden, if the lady and gentleman wish to take their tea in the garden . . ." I decided that if the shaking of her breasts could be stopped, some of the fragments of the afternoon might be collected, and I concentrated my attention with careful subtlety to this end.

Even at this early stage, Eliot is by nature a presentative poet. The scene is a thoroughly embarrassing one, and one's first impression is that Eliot is handling it by being perfectly objective—that is, by focusing entirely on moment-by-moment sense impressions: the hysterical woman's teeth as she laughs uncontrollably, and the view down the tunnel of her throat, the appearance of the waiter, the neutral details concerning the table and the tablecloth, and the shaking of the woman's breasts. But one soon notices that these external data are, as it were, a constant of the poem. What actually unfolds is the speaker's own state.

At first he is passively engulfed by the shock of what is happening. He "was aware" that he was "being involved" and made a "part" of the woman's behavior—not her feeling but what is happening to her body. His own perturbation is not stated but projected by way of images for what he is observing. The image, for example, of the woman's teeth as "accidental stars with a talent for squad-drill" is not merely clever but a suggestion of the cosmos in disorder—or reordered to reflect hysteria. Similarly, the waiter's "trembling hands" and his nervous repetitions are a displaced expression of the speaker's state of mind after he has been "drawn in," "inhaled," and "bruised" by the woman's rhythm of laughter, gasps, and "momentary recovery." It is the man, then, who is *bruised* by the experience in this poem—"bruised" is the one word that directly expresses pain—and it is he who takes action of a sort at the end, to bring an end to his disturbed state by stopping "the shaking of her breasts"—the most striking displacement of all.

If this is comedy of embarrassment, the ending almost succeeds in its effort to be *purely* comic, for it fixes attention with a mad single-mindedness on something no man could avoid thinking of doing even while he could hardly allow himself the thought of doing it—namely, seizing the breasts and making them be still by main force. Leaving aside the somewhat suspect matter of the speaker's attitude toward the woman, who is a condition of the poem rather than a person in her own right and who provides only one instance among many of Eliot's poetic oppression by the burdens of female physicality and female hysteria, we have an early instance here of his superb buffoonery. It is the buffoonery of a sensibility with more feeling than it can express directly—the artistic problem discussed in Eliot's best critical essay, "Hamlet and His Problems." Rereading once again, one can see that "Hysteria" crams into its second sentence a great deal of active language that is not only sexual in its suggestiveness (another "displacement" of reference) but also alive with reverse birth-imagery. It is literally true that more is going on here than the speaker can handle. The title goes beyond the immediate dramatic situation. It implies preoccupation with everything specifically female and related to the womb. Something the speaker has said or done, some failure of sympathy in any case, has presumably led to the woman's outburst; but also, the language implies, the female principle itself is something the speaker cannot face without losing his self-possession. The comic ending forestalls further exploration in this poem, but not of course in others.

One of these others is the poem "Ode," which in *Ara Vos Prec* was substituted for "Hysteria" but then replaced by it again in subsequent collected editions. Many of the elements of "Hysteria" are present in this poem which is at once more confessional and less direct. Humor here is entirely absorbed into irony and into a feeling of bitter incongruity between fantasies of ritual sexual initiation derived from myth and literature and the letdown of an unhappy first experience by a newly married couple. The opening stanzas each begin with a word for the situation and specifically for the bridegroom's feelings—the first with "Tired," the second with "Misunderstood," the third with "Tortured." It is the third stanza which reveals the literal scene amidst sardonic notes of fruitfulness and celebration:

> Tortured.
> When the bridegroom smoothed his hair
> There was blood upon the bed.
> Morning was already late.
> Children singing in the orchard
> (Io Hymen, Hymenaee)
> Succuba eviscerate.

The welter of mythological reference and subtle indirection in the closing stanza is appropriately introduced by the word "Tortuous." The speaker compares his letdown to "the fooled resentment of the dragon" from whom Perseus rescued Andromeda and ends the poem with phrasing somewhat anticipatory of *Hugh Selwyn Mauberley*, published a few months later.

> Indignant
> At the cheap extinction of his taking-off
> Now lies he there
> Tip to tip washed beneath Charles' Wagon.

Eliot restored "Hysteria" and dropped "Ode" in the American edition (*Poems*) and thereafter. The unpleasant personal reference and generally whining tone were probably the reason. Also, "Hysteria" is certainly the better poem, having none of the involuted, somewhat repetitious allusiveness of "Ode" and managing its self-consciousness far more effectively through its simple dramatic details, energetic language, and manically natural ending. Nevertheless, this rejected poem has a strong underlying authority. It struggles with frustration and self-loathing, the horror of being mocked by whatever counts in life and faith: "subterrene laughter synchronous / With silence from the sacred wood." It confronts, however overallusively, a feeling of failure of which the marriage-bed fiasco is but one token. And it risks having

the speaker see his small private grief against a back-
ground of heroic tradition and universal significance. In
short, it is more ambitious than "Hysteria" and far from
adequate to its task, and yet moves into position for it.
Only two years later, in "The Waste Land," Eliot gives
this task the room it needs, partly by employing the virtues of "Hysteria" on a much larger canvas but also by
facing into the sense of psychological reality foreshadowed in "Ode."

A failure like this one is more the sign of the artist
than any number of minor formal successes. The struggle
for form is not to write something that will be thought
attractive by the general reader but to awaken realization
of a felt state, in language adequate to the need. Formal
structure, in this exploratory, improvisatory sense, is
always open, a venture at risk. The poet needs to convey
a subjective condition by composing a music of feeling
in language; he does not quite know what he is set to
convey until his own phrasing realizes into it. So a certain number of tentative starts is ordinarily required
along the way, before he can see the scale he is really
working on. Eliot's instinct for this process was probably
the keenest of any poet writing in our language in this
century.

How tentative, how open the process is could always
be discerned by poets engaged in their art in a keen
enough way. The recovery of the lost version of "The
Waste Land"—"the original drafts including the annotations of Ezra Pound" reproduced in the Valerie Eliot edition of 1971*—was extremely useful in demonstrating
this crucial characteristic of poetry. It compelled a new

*T. S. Eliot, *The Waste Land: A Facsimile and Transcript of the Original Drafts
Including the Annotations of Ezra Pound,* edited and with an introduction by
Valerie Eliot (New York: Harcourt Brace Jovanovich, 1971).

recognition, at once, of the open character of that poem's structure. I do not mean that the earlier drafts show us what Eliot was "really" doing in the final one; only the text a poet decides to remain with takes the responsibility for itself. But because of certain emphases while the poem was still in the making, the sense of improvisation at the high pitch of genius that struck the first readers of the printed text is reinforced.

Pound was more than helpful while Eliot was making his decisions, as the Valerie Eliot edition demonstrates. But one almost does well to forget this direct editorial cooperation, which is of the sort poets have often given one another, and think in quite other terms: Pound's own improvisatory tacks, for example, or D. H. Lawrence's insight into Whitman as the poet of the "open road" and of himself as writing "poetry of the present." Lawrence wrote, in 1918, of "the poetry of that which is at hand: the immediate present. In the immediate present there is no perfection, no consummation, nothing finished. The strands are all flying, quivering, intermingling into the web, the waters shaking the moon. . . . This is the unrestful, ungraspable poetry of the sheer present, poetry whose very permanency lies in its wind-like transit." This was in Lawrence's introduction to the American edition of his *New Poems*. But five years earlier still he had written, in a letter: "I have always tried to get an emotion out in its own course, without altering it. It needs the finest instinct imaginable, much finer than the skill of craftsmen."

Eliot was a poetic craftsman beyond Lawrence's ability to grasp, but what Lawrence says here is most important. One could assemble a huge battery of statements by him and others, even by Pound and Eliot, to show how much a renewed fascination with the organic and "wind-harp" conceptions of Romantic poetics affected the young avant-garde poets and theorists of the time. Eliot made something of a show of intellectual rigor in his criticism—his learning and classicism and formal self-discipline. Yet he too was infected with the desire to write directly out of the "immediate present," to use the language and the experience and the whole context of life that was "at hand." To isolate, release, recognize, and ride the real emotional direction of the poem—such an aim involves the sense of improvisation at the pitch of genius I have mentioned. The true poem, in this perspective, consists of a series of affects that together create its life. Their order is a tentative satisfying of the ultimately unsatisfiable need to explore the emotional range they embody. In his essay on Marlowe, Eliot observes that "the blank verse of Tennyson . . . is cruder (*not* 'rougher' or less perfect in technique) than that of half a dozen contemporaries of Shakespeare; cruder, because less capable of expressing complicated, subtle, and surprising emotions." In his essay on *Hamlet,* he points out—it is his most telling comment, and absolutely pertinent to his own work—the importance for Shakespeare of one psychological reality: "The intense feeling, ecstatic or terrible, without an object or exceeding its object, is something which every person of sensibility has known. . . ." This is Lawrence's idea in a more sophisticated form.

It is therefore not surprising that Eliot, in the face of his preoccupations in "The Waste Land" with some rather large moral, religious, and social issues, and with philosophical and cultural meanings of a very inclusive kind, should have reacted nevertheless against people's ignoring the feeling at the center of it: "To me it was only the relief of a personal and wholly insignificant grouse about life; it is just a piece of rhythmic grum-

bling."* The broad and deep preoccupations I have mentioned are certainly present and even enable us to see a
clear rhetorical progression in the poem. But they are not
the point of the poem. They are only dimensions of the
speaking consciousness. If it seems difficult to reconcile
Eliot's "rhythmic grumbling" comment with his elaborate footnotes to the poem, one must remember that the
poem is primary. The notes show us a great many sub-
jects that the poet was interested in, refer us to books he
had read, and introduce specific observations on the
text, but they are not after all the poem. From this viewpoint, the comment I have quoted is finally just another
note. And there is no reason we cannot be instructed by
any of the notes if only it is immediately related to what
is going on in the poem's actual language.

I should like to follow this thought a little further, by
quoting both a key passage in the poem (lines 412–17)
and Eliot's notes accompanying it and then by pausing
over the relationship. The passage:

> I have heard the key
> Turn in the door once and turn once only
> We think of the key, each in his prison
> Thinking of the key, each confirms a prison
> Only at nightfall, aethereal rumours
> Revive for a moment a broken Coriolanus.

The notes to this passage are provided without comment:

> Cf. *Inferno*, XXXIII, 46:

> "ed io sentii chiavar l'uscio di sotto
> all 'orribile torre."

> ["and down below I heard them nailing up the door
> of the horrible tower."]

* Quoted in the Valerie Eliot edition, p. xiii.

Also F. H. Bradley, *Appearance and Reality*, p. 346.

"My external sensations are no less private to myself than
are my thoughts or my feelings. In either case my experience falls within my own circle, a circle closed on the outside; and with all its elements alike, every sphere is
opaque to the others which surround it. . . . In brief,
regarded as an existence which appears in a soul, the
whole world for each is peculiar and private to that soul."

Now, neither of these quotations that Eliot gives us to
be ranged alongside the lines I have quoted from "The
Waste Land" *explains* the lines or accounts for their presence. Each, however, is cognate with them. The first
refers to the moment in the *Inferno* when Ugolino,
imprisoned with his sons in the Tower of Hunger,
awakes to find they are being sealed into the place forever. Nothing in Eliot's lines evokes the specific Dantean
reference in itself, let alone the full hideousness of the
Ugolino tale. Moreover, the allusion to Coriolanus in the
passage itself takes us in a quite different direction. But
the two lines from Dante show us that Eliot associates
them, in the wind-harp music of his own sensibility,
with the terror of a soul imprisoned in itself. Only if we
permit ourselves to consider the notes an integral part of
the essential text, like the documentary material which
Pound, William Carlos Williams, and many others today
incorporate into the fabric of a developing work, can we
do more than nod sympathetically at the poet's giving us
a favorite quotation by someone else to nudge us into
seeing his poem a certain way.

The Dante quotation brings in a powerful affect from
outside the poem to light our way somehow. The quotation from F. H. Bradley introduces a philosophical concept to which, as it happens, the poet had given a great
deal of thought. He had written his doctoral dissertation

on Bradley's theory of "Immediate Experience" as the ambiguous, undifferentiated condition of the living self in the midst of its world, hardly sorted out from the reality engulfing and saturating it. This idea is embodied in the quotation Eliot provides, although the emphasis there is on the imprisonment of the self within the undifferentiated context of its "immediate" existence. Again, it is important to note, what Bradley says is hardly what Eliot's own lines evoke. The Bradleyan approach, indeed, implies for the poet a continuously depressive condition that was not at all the concern of the philosopher: a state in which the psyche is so invaded and possessed by "outside" reality that it cannot define itself and its purposes in any actively formed perspective. The combination of the two starting points, the philosopher's and the poet's, suggests the condition of psychic readiness poetry strives for rather than a gloss of a particular passage in "The Waste Land."

We have noticed how lyric poems exist within such a state in at least two poems, Pound's Canto 47 and Yeats's "All Souls' Night." Poetically speaking, this is the state of readiness shared by the poet and his work—readiness to receive the unavoidable impact of reality and readiness to move out of this open and vulnerable position into the exploration of possible new sets of attitude and awareness. The characteristic lyric poem of the past two centuries begins with recognition of a real situation that has perhaps elusively melancholy overtones, or with a direct statement of a feeling of sadness or precarious balance. It moves into a sense of the complexity of the relationships and feelings it is contemplating, often marked by a sense of confusion and of the breaking down of normal distinctions. It ends with something like reconciliation, but on closer examination the reconciliation consists in the speaker's recognition of a drastically and tragically unchangeable reality. Paradoxically, this recognition has the ring of a joyous affirmation. Eliot's "Shantih shantih shantih," which picks up from his gloriously elated language of ascetic abnegation (like the closing stanza of Yeats's "Demon and Beast"), is but one of a very long series that would include such endings as Wallace Stevens's "Downward to darkness on extended wings" and Yeats's

> Hermits upon Mount Meru or Everest,
> Caverned in night under the drifted snow,
> Or where that snow and winter's dreadful blast
> Beat down upon their naked bodies, know
> That day brings round the night, that before dawn
> His glory and his monuments are gone.

The movement, in other words, is from a state of depressive awareness to one of depressive transcendence. It is not usually a straight-line movement, particularly in a sequence; except in relatively short pieces, it tends to be a series of balancings. The total flux of aroused awareness is a condition of the whole poem—a set of possibilities, not a purposeful fiction or argument. Within this flux the depressive state inseparable from a sufficiently open sensibility is countered by momentary holdings against the chaos threatening the speaker from both without and within. A lyric poem is, in this way of seeing it, a sensibility in motion. The motion is toward a tentative reconciliation by way of a number of poised balancings interspersed among movements of loss and dissolution. These balancings hold off absolute loss of morale, if only through the purity with which a negative recognition is evoked and sustained. Let me again cite lines 412–17:

> I have heard the key
> Turn in the door once and turn once only

> We think of the key, each in his prison
> Thinking of the key, each confirms a prison
> Only at nightfall, aetherial rumours
> Revive for a moment a broken Coriolanus.

The passage presents sharp and striking images for the speaker's spiritual isolation and vague, distant sense of defeated pride. At the same time, it has positive tonalities mostly contradicted by the literal context. I say "mostly" because the image of a key that locks one into oneself does not exclude the possibility of the key's being turned the other way. Also, there are associations of transcendence and tragic heroism implicit in the "aetherial rumours" that "revive," if only "for a moment," even a "broken Coriolanus." This is a balancing, though on the whole negative in its implications. Another "positive" tonality is created by the word "confirms," though what is being confirmed is "a prison." The music of the passage sustains its balancings of motifs and tones. The confessional voice at the start, followed by the meditative voice that shifts from "I" to "we" and then by the exalted melancholy of the closing two lines, introduces a play on the word "key" that induces contemplation of its varied suggestiveness. This is done partly through sheer repetition and partly because "key" is alliterative with "confirms" and "Coriolanus" and has an insistent vowel echoed in "we" and in "aetherial." By the time the passage closes we are thinking of "keys" to the poem's psychological frustrations and to its largest possible meanings as against the dead pressure of a continuum of undifferentiated reality.*

In its formal movement the passage epitomizes "The

---

*See Richard Wollheim's excellent "Eliot and F. H. Bradley: An Account," in Graham Martin, ed., *Eliot in Perspective: A Symposium* (New York: Humanities Press, 1970). Wollheim takes up this passage, but without regard to its poetic character.

Waste Land" as a whole. Its final balance is not really final at all. It is a precarious stay against breakdown, a set of notes that might easily enough be extended with other groups of images. In fact, the next six lines do just that, brilliantly; and the next eleven lines, which end the poem, do so once again. Those final eleven lines, too, "handle" the problem projected at the beginning of the poem by jumbling together the basic tonalities of morale that punctuate the whole work. These are, in order of appearance, the breakdown in madness and meaninglessness that comes with loss of sustaining vision; the passion to search out purification by discipline and mortification; the inseparable linking of tragedy and transporting desire in mythical and literary tradition; the emptiness felt by the speaker himself (coming forward, at last, as the poet who has "shored" the "fragments" of which the poem is made "against my ruins"); and the counter-motifs of spiritual redemption and calm at the end, themselves concealed as nonsense words until the English-speaking reader is properly indoctrinated: an ironic stylistic balance of some importance.

The poem no more necessarily ends here than at several other places. Its real movement is of brief, irregularly alternating cycles of depressive letdown and of resistance to it. In Lawrence's words, Eliot "gets an emotion out in its own course, without altering it." He lets himself be carried by it but improvises ways of coping with it. For the "emotion" is actually a complex of feelings and attitudes informing what he later downgraded, half-humorously, as the "personal and wholly insignificant grouse against life" that he used the poem to "relieve."

Not to go into too tedious detail, we may trace the alternations of affect that define the progress of "The Burial of the Dead," and then add a few notes about later sections. The exquisite and poignant music of the first four lines, with their vital and painful challenge to meet the self-renewing demands of life, has a curious echo without resonance in the ensuing three lines. These are deliberately dulled and casually diffident in tone though they sustain the participial rhyming and general rhythmic character of the opening. Marie's expanded, more relaxed lines provide another kind of echo of the opening. Memory and desire are evoked once more, but are rendered trivial by the life-patterns within which they are held; the loose rhythm of the opening of this section, and the anticlimactic ending, make Marie's speech that of one of the dull roots of lines 4–7. If one still feels a certain bravery and touching love of excitement in what she says, the deeper voice of lines 19–30, deprecating such roots and branches as could possibly grow "out of this stony rubbish," introduces the sound of prophetic horror at human reality seen in its terrifyingly amoral emptiness. The new voice's compulsive repetitions balance this terror at our loss against the promise of a revelation that may be yet more terrible. Then the music of rhetorical prophetic insistence drops away. It was another reverberation, we should note, of the atmosphere of challenge suggested in the opening lines, and even of their romantic intensity. But now something more similarly evocative of the world of erotic desire and its full implication of painful self-awareness reenters the poem in the lines from *Tristan und Isolde* and in the "hyacinth girl" passage. Madame Sosostris, another dull root, presents a welcome comic and satiric variation while introducing themes from the deeper world of prophetic mystery though she does not understand them. At last, in its turn, the "Unreal City" passage (one of the three or four most powerful and concentrated climactic points in the whole sequence) transposes the comic and satirical effects to something grimly fantastic and grotesque and appalled.

My point is that we have been carried through a process of emotional clarification that is musically ordered, a music of feeling rather than a music of ideas, its dynamics determined by shifts in the intensity and lyric deployment of the successive passages. Attraction to life's most magnetic sources in body and spirit vies with fear of its consequences in the opening lines, and all the ensuing variations and modulations and transpositions open out and narrow down this central, active motive caught into the poem by the opening words. "April is the cruellest month . . .." The two opposed sets of dramatic speech, one hysterically inward and the other savagely comic and externalized, of "A Game of Chess" provide yet another context for the same polar oppositions. Richness, then sheer need and distraction of spirit, then sardonic notes that pick up from those concealed in the serious Shakespearian parody at the start, then jazzy rhythms like those in Madame Sosostris's speech, then the chill paralysis of the sheer failure of feeling, and then the protracted, complex mixture of low comedy, desperate grossness, and doomsday warning—these are, on the whole, the dominant succeeding affects here. Still "mixing memory and desire" and the fear of pain and of barrenness with both, the poem's genius lies in its prolificacy of variations and of new tones that yet are controlled by the one original emotional complex with which it began. The possibilities for more and more variation, with a cumulative effect so long as redundancy is avoided and the extent of the poem does not stifle the emotion, are not inexhaustible although the limits of the power of any given sequence are easier to discern than to characterize.

In any case, the extraordinary stylistic variations, and in particular the varied lyric forms that interact with one another within this poetic constellation and yet remain superbly independent, are what make this poem the unique achievement it is. The possibilities of the initial emotion are realized in a large number of directions within the same magnetic field. The Bradleyan perspective serves the poet as a reminder of the gulf between what we can actually know and the self-transcendence to which we aspire. It makes any state of awareness keyed to sharply defined insight (as opposed to passive immersion in experience) in some sense an affirmation. States of ecstasy and horror can in this sense be balanced on one side of the scale against sheer entropy. It can, I think, be argued—though to demonstrate in detail would take many pages—that "The Waste Land" despite some aberrations proceeds through purer and purer intensities to extend and weigh the polarities with which it begins, but that it need not necessarily have stopped where it did. The surface rhetoric is in this sense an interference with the real process of the poem.

Recovery of the earlier drafts shows us what some of the alternative possibilities were. One needs to be open, not only to the deleted passages as given to us in the Valerie Eliot edition, but also to the possibilities they represent. Whatever, for instance, one may think of the original first section of "He Do the Police in Different Voices," it is important to remember that its very presence would have changed the character of the whole poem and that Eliot would probably have revised and developed it differently in a final draft had he decided to keep it—as he did, say, with the Tiresias passage whose first line originally read: "The typist home at teatime, who begins. . .." To start "The Burial of the Dead" ("He Do the Police in Different Voices: Part I") with the long account of a night out in Boston was a more daring idea than has been recognized. It got the sequence off in low

gear rather than at the highly concentrated lyric pitch of
the present opening. Thus the poem would have lacked
the advantage of an initial powerful center of reference
around which the rest of the sections would appear to be
developed. On the other hand, the idea of establishing a
context of colloquialism and of commonplace urban life
from the start had its own advantages:

> First we had a couple of feelers down at Tom's place,
> There was old Tom, boiled to the eyes, blind . . .

The idiom becomes more specifically American a bit further on, and at the same time introduces the sexual
theme without the romantic and emotional force it takes
on a little later in the poem:

—("I turned up an hour later down at Myrtle's place.
What d'y'mean, she says, at two o'clock in the morning,
I'm not in business here for guys like you;
We've only had a raid last week. I've been warned twice.

All this was difficult to manage, technically. Eliot had
to get Boston Irish speech right, and also the normal hes-
itations and crude phrasing of most uncultivated conversation. Perhaps he meant to mingle the diction of college
students with that of Myrtle and the local Irish-American
speech. The cadences are abrupt though syncopated, and
the allusions to current songs and Boston places are almost parochial. It is easy to dismiss what he does here,
and yet the modulation toward a genuine poetry based
on the speech of the streets is suggestive of a possibility
for which the poetic situation was on the whole not yet
ready. An atmosphere of casual and commercialized li-
centiousness is quickly established, as trivial and yet as
cheating to the protagonist's real desires as the life of
Marie. A certain ambience of confusion is established
too. The love of music, theatre, erotic experience, and
joy for its own sake, and the importance of magnanim-

ity, are set forward as values despite the vulgarity of their manifestations. At the end of the passage the protagonist separates himself from the others—"I got out to see the sunrise, and walked home." It is the beginning of the journey among the levels of feeling and of moral condition that "The Waste Land" reports. And suddenly, in the next passage, we are reading: "April is the cruellest month . . .." The shift is a wrenching one, between extremes that mark out the opposite poles of consciousness in the poem. This was surely a potentially fruitful direction of the poem, one that might have informed it with a dimension of ordinary reality had the orientation been somewhat different.

In this context, the original beginning of "Death by Water," with its knowledgeable depiction of the life of sailors and the circumstances of serving on old sailing ships, also linked common experience with the larger motifs of the sequence. It is extremely interesting to see Eliot employing materials not unlike Masefield's while sustaining a highly formal precision of language in his own right and at the same time writing with a candor and a deliberate interrupting of the formal tone that foreshadows the method of a poet like Charles Olson:

> The sailor, attentive to the chart and to the sheets,
> A concentrated will against the tempest and the tide,
> Retains, even ashore, in public bars or streets
> Something inhuman, clean, and dignified.
>
> Even the drunken ruffian who descends
> Illicit backstreet stairs, to reappear,
> For the derision of his sober friends,
> Staggering, or limping with a comic gonorrhea,
>
> From his trade with wind and sea and snow, as they
> Are, he is, with "much seen and much endured,"
> Foolish, impersonal, innocent or gay,
> Liking to be shaved, combed, scented, manicured.

Elimination of this passage, and of the account of a ship's strange and sinister journey that follows, left only the brief Phlebas the Phoenician passage as Part IV. As with the deletion of the original opening lines of the poem, what was retained made for greater emphasis and clearer outlines. Yet if both passages had been retained, at the beginnings of "The Burial of the Dead" and of "Death by Water," they would have constituted a continuing journey or quest pattern that would have prepared the reader for the Grail motif of "What the Thunder Said." The loose, halting rhythms of the deleted passage at the start were to be replaced by the firmer ones of the passage on the sailors' journey. Tragic proportion would thereby have been lent to the common life as we saw the sailors inexorably having to face their fate under a supernatural compulsion. The speaker's yearning toward that common life is now suggested only incidentally in a few lines of the poem. With retention of these two passages, it would have entered the poem's music more penetratingly whatever the effect on the total balance of the poem would have been.

Finally, had Eliot retained the "Fresca" passage originally at the head of "The Fire Sermon" and kept certain omitted lines about the "young man carbuncular" in the passage about the typist's seduction, a strong personal note of disgust and contempt would have altered the whole atmosphere of *The Waste Land*. His Swiftian revulsion at Fresca, the chic, vulgar female poetaster at her toilet and in society, violates the generous and emotionally open sensibility that seems to preside, otherwise, over most of the poem. A pettiness and meanness pervades the satire here, and the wit dissipates itself against a hardly formidable victim. That "Fresca slips softly to the needful stool" is hardly a powerful satirical point, and the following lines about her seem pathologically inflamed:

> This ended, to her steaming bath she moves,
> Her tresses fanned by little flutt'ring Loves;
> Odours, confected by the artful French,
> Disguise the good old hearty female stench.

These lines, and much of the rest that goes with them, give a bitchy flavor to Eliot's style that carries over to the scenes in "A Game of Chess" and to other scenes elsewhere in the poem. If retained, they would have destroyed the fine distancing generally maintained between the ultimate voice of the poem and the characters seen in closeup. Similarly, the contempt shown toward the young man and the typist in the original draft for their cultural pretensions obscures the essential bearing of the scene that depends in part on their viciousness being seen as ignorant and even innocent. And yet Eliot, had he kept these passages, would have committed himself to a much more confessional and vulnerable role in the structure of the poem. He would have had to set his own finicky and precious attitudes, and his abysmal feelings about female physicality, into the scale with other predominant motifs. These were possibilities of commitment toward which he went a fairly long way. In the era of Robert Lowell and Allen Ginsberg, he might well have gone the whole distance. Neither his nor Pound's taste was ready to be confident about doing so in 1922, and doubtless the best available reading public for poetry would not have been ready either. When he wrote, in the typist's seduction scene, that the young man

> Bestows one final patronising kiss,
> And gropes his way, finding the stairs unlit;
> And at the corner where the stable is,
> Delays only to urinate, and spit,

Pound crossed out the last two lines and wrote in the margin: "probably over the mark."

So "The Waste Land" is an open structure in two senses. The first sense is the one developed at the start of this discussion, and has to do with the dynamics of the poem's movement as an extended lyric structure in sequence form. The structural principle resides not in ideas but in affects within a float of memories and associations in an ambiguous realm of consciousness, their direction determined by a driving emotional preoccupation. Intensities and modes of language define the structure; no story ends or argument completes itself here, but a momentary sense of balance provides a tentative sense of closure now and then.

The second kind of openness lies in the undeveloped potentialities suggested by excised portions of the earlier draft. We have not looked at all those passages, but have noted enough to show that certain colloquial modes of verse, and certain unattractive dimensions of personal feeling, were suppressed in the interests of an advanced poetics that was nevertheless not yet ready for them in the early 1920s. The feelings of the desired audience were a factor as well, as Pound's comment that I have just quoted would seem to indicate. A definite critical success was sought for "The Waste Land," and that fact, and the two poets' stage of development at just that point, and Eliot's nervous condition all militated toward the inhibition of certain lines of exploration. Every poem is after all open in the sense that it could be developed further, it could be improved, if only the poet's energies and state of readiness were a trifle beyond their actual state. But "The Waste Land," because of its place in the history of modern poetry and the peculiar history of its text, and because of its pioneering inward voyage by way of externalized images and other points of reference, is a particularly fascinating instance and problem.

Eliot never again matched the combined richness, volatility, and dance of voices in "The Waste Land." His plays, for all their wit and happier *aperçus* and occasional other felicities, never approach the dramatic vivacity of this poem. *Murder in the Cathedral* probably comes closest. It has some of the archaic force of Greek tragedy and of the morality play. Also, its waves of choral chanting put the violence, the saintly courage, and the ambiguities brought out by the main speeches and actions in direct touch with the anxious foreboding of humble folk whose destinies depend on the power struggle the play ritualizes.

Still, after "The Waste Land," Eliot explored more fully certain veins of feeling and vision and psychologically precarious states the earlier poetry had introduced. The association of an ambience of "magic" or "glamor" with states of suffering is strongly evident in his work from the start: an atmosphere at once saturated with a complex nostalgia, which is darkened by shame, fear, and the grip of an unwilling coldness, and unstable because of a sadistic warp. "The Love Song of J. Alfred Prufrock" cannot quite, it is true, be described in these terms, but its music of lonely regression suggests a passive or masochistic obverse of poems like "Portrait of a Lady" and "La Figlia che Piange." In those early pieces (in *Prufrock* and *Poems*) the impression of a speaking character and the impression of the empirical world in which he exists are inseparable—

> Shall I say, I have gone at dusk through narrow streets
> And watched the smoke that rises from the pipes
> Of lonely men in shirt-sleeves, leaning out of windows? . . .

or:

> Now that lilacs are in bloom
> She has a bowl of lilacs in her room
> And twists one in her fingers while she talks.

"Ah, my friend, you do not know, you do not know
What life is, you who hold it in your hands" . . .

I take my hat: how can I make a cowardly amends
For what she has said to me?
You will see me any morning in the park
Reading the comics and the sporting page.
Particularly I remark
An English countess goes upon the stage.
A Greek was murdered at a Polish dance,
Another bank defaulter has confessed.
I keep my countenance,
I remain self-possessed
Except when a street piano, mechanical and tired
Reiterates some worn-out common song
With the smell of hyacinths across the garden
Recalling things that other people have desired.
Are these ideas right or wrong?

or, most especially:

Stand on the highest pavement of the stair—
Lean on a garden urn—
Weave, weave the sunlight in your hair—
Clasp your flowers to you with a pained surprise—
Fling them to the ground and turn
With a fugitive resentment in your eyes:
But weave, weave the sunlight in your hair.

So I would have had him leave,
So I would have had her stand and grieve,
So he would have left
As the soul leaves the body torn and bruised,
As the mind deserts the body it has used.
I should find
Some way incomparably light and deft,
Some way we both should understand,
Simple and faithless as a smile and shake of the hand.

These quotations are all from the first book, from "Prufrock," "Portrait of a Lady," and "La Figlia che Piange" respectively. Together with "Preludes" and the very bitter, morbidly beautiful "Rhapsody on a Windy Night," these are the most accomplished earliest poems. All are lyric poems whose control of patterned sound and rhythm is exquisitely sure in its suggestion of traditional poetic structure while the form itself is actually varied and highly improvisational, a free musical composition based on the changing needs of the emotional context. For instance, the phrasing, the repetitions, the use of rhyme, and the interweaving of longer and shorter lines in the two stanzas from "La Figlia che Piange" are similar; yet the stanzas are of different length, the rhymes fall at different intervals, and the closing line of the second stanza violates our expectations even within the loose patterning so far observed. The sudden change has to do with the shift in tone between the stanzas. The first is an ambiguous but intensely felt appreciation of a scene observed or remembered, whether in literal reality or in a painting or perhaps in imagination. It has acutely romantic, even erotic aspects, and a certain cruelty in the approving imperatives of lines four and five. The second, with its conditional verb forms, is more distanced and speculative in one sense, more coolly but diabolically involved in another. The first two lines echo the feeling of the first stanza, the next few introduce very violent imagery that heightens the sense of a cruelly passionate imagination (or one struggling to arouse itself through violent and desolate images), and the four closing lines introduce the thought of the speaker as participant—a self-possessed and "faithless" lover. The ambiguity of the whole situation of the poem makes it impossible to place the relationships explicitly, but there is a dream of triumphant infliction of pain here, underlined by the unusually long closing line with its flat-out cynicism of tone.

Similar elements are present in the speaker's presentation of himself as devoid of any capacity for passionate feeling in "Gerontion," the *chef d'œuvre* of *Poems*. "Gerontion" is subtler and more complex than anything in *Prufrock,* but its atmospheric density and intense yearning for the ability to *be* intense at any cost give it a family resemblance to the poems already cited. Eliot's liberal use of the feverish, insinuating rhythms of Jacobean tragic drama, his restless characters who violate the great human mysteries but have their seductive side, and his protagonist's sudden confessional anguish in the climactic stanza beginning "The tiger springs in the new year" are signs of a great advance in his artistic copiousness and resourcefulness. He was able to work now on a larger scale, with more active elements in motion at the same time in a poem, and more surprisingly, than before. Work on "Gerontion" and on "The Waste Land" began at about the same time, and in both instances we have the introduction of Christian references as elements in the emotional life of the poem. Modern skeptical refusal of faith is opposed to openhearted readiness for it; both works involve this opposition in the emotional predicament (an inner storm that takes the form of terror at being or becoming a dead soul) on which the dynamics of each is based.

Such an opposition is in itself nothing very new in poetry, quite obviously. The artistic issue for Eliot was to remain the lyric poet he started out to be, and to assimilate religious consciousness to it by way of nerve-endings, not doctrinal points. In my earlier chapter on "Little Gidding" I discussed the difficulties he faced in that poem as well as its achievement, and we shall return to

Four Quartets a bit further on. The problem emerged strikingly in "Gerontion" and "The Waste Land," but made itself felt as an aspect of the speaker's neurotic range of awareness, the phantasmagoria, images, memories, and impulses of feeling that he wanted to bring into ordered balance. The sense of crisis is so acute, especially in "The Waste Land," that although the poems include potentially intractable religious positions they remain inviolate. One cannot distinguish the speaking sensibility from its Christian orientation any more than from the other dimensions of its thought and its suffering. Eliot's primary center of reference, as a poet, remains "the intense feeling, ecstatic or terrible, without an object or exceeding its object" that is the real subject of his *Hamlet* essay and the heart of his poems. The deep early involvement with Bradley's "Immediate Experience" is a reflex of this essential inner preoccupation.

The evolution and the final form of "The Hollow Men" demonstrate Eliot's instinct, as a poet, for finding the lyrical correlative for his intellectual and religious quarrels with himself. The "inner storm" that is "The Waste Land" flings into view a multitude of points of emotive reference in the struggle against the anomie paradoxically accompanying the speaker's "intense feeling." "The Hollow Men" may be viewed as a shaking down of the same poetic materials to the end of sorting out their basic psychic tone. It is interesting that originally the first part of this five-part poem was published independently, and that in the same year (1924) the third part appeared as the concluding poem in a small sequence called "Doris's Dream Songs." Part I, by itself, consists of three brief movements. The first stanza is a perfect rendition of an elaborated oxymoron for the paradoxical state I have mentioned. The way that Eliot brings in the tiny outcry "Alas!" to point up the intensity (a "comic" anguish comparable with that in the opening stanza of "The Tower") is but one sign of his almost infallible ear at this point in his career:

> We are the hollow men
> We are the stuffed men
> Leaning together
> Headpiece filled with straw. Alas!
> Our dried voices, when
> We whisper together
> Are quiet and meaningless
> As wind in dry grass
> Or rats' feet over broken glass
> In our dry cellar

After this superb beginning the next stanza provides a whole series of relatively abstract oxymora in two lines that somewhat dull the impact of all the dry, rustling, whispering, sad strangeness of the opening stanza. The one word "paralyzed" (with its plosive effect that contradicts its meaning) calls attention to a psychological state implied but not emphasized earlier on. The closing stanza then abruptly introduces an entirely new set of associations, religious in character, that break the self-entrancement of the poem. Two images, "with direct eyes" and "lost / Violent souls," quicken this ending but cannot prevent its somewhat contrived effect of doing too much too quickly and too bluntly:

> Shape without form, shade without colour,
> Paralyzed force, gesture without motion;
>
> Those who have crossed
> With direct eyes, to death's other Kingdom
> Remember us—if at all—not as lost
> Violent souls, but only
> As the hollow men
> The stuffed men.

Originally titled "Poème," these stanzas were published together with a translation by St.-J. Perse in the Winter 1924–25 issue of the Parisian magazine *Commerce*. In reflex conjunction with its French mirror-image it has a serendipitously magnetic effect; but taken by itself it is not quite realized despite the extraordinary opening and the suggestive power of most of the final stanza. The ambiguity of "crossed . . . to death's other Kingdom" sets the responsive imagination wondering, and the image of "direct eyes" is striking but, in context, turned away from the speakers. It is easy to say that more was needed, since Eliot did add more in the final version. But as I have already suggested, sometimes he could add too much in order to point himself and the reader the "right" way. "Poème" is very short, yet in a sense it is too long because the ending attempts to impose its tendentious frame, however tactfully, with a sudden rush.

Almost simultaneously Part III of the final version of "The Hollow Men" appeared in the *Chapbook* of November 1924 as the last poem in "Doris's Dream Songs." This sequence began with "Eyes that last I saw in tears" and "The wind sprang up at four o'clock." (The two poems now head the section called "Minor Poems" in collected editions of the poetry.) The first is a poem of remorse, loss, and guilt without referent; the second is a poem of death-fear and, again, terrible remorse without a referent (somewhat akin to Joyce's "I hear an army charging"). However, "This is the dead land" has the most personal immediacy of the three because of the stark loneliness it presents in lines nine through eleven. It has the same function in its present position at the center of "The Hollow Men," where its plaintive questioning makes it the fulcrum between the fears and velleities of the first two parts and the more decisive visions of the final two parts.

This is the dead land
This is cactus land
Here the stone images
Are raised, here they receive
The supplication of a dead man's hand
Under the twinkle of a fading star.

Is it like this
In death's other kingdom
Waking alone
At the hour when we are
Trembling with tenderness
Lips that would kiss
Form prayers to broken stone.

From the viewpoint of lyric concentration "Doris's Dream Songs" catch the essential anguish floating in the unconscious mind (as suggested by the phrase "dream songs") more purely than does "The Hollow Men." One can only speculate that Eliot found its range too narrow for his conscious purpose. Perhaps, too, he found that ending "Doris's Dream Songs" with "This is the dead land" made the group too obvious an afterbeat of "The Waste Land." At any rate, he quickly shifted the balance of things in "The Hollow Men." A more developed short sequence than "Doris's Dream Songs," this opens with "We are the hollow men" and has the clearly reciprocal "This is the dead land" at its center. This altered position changes its emphasis slightly, so that the lines "Waking alone / At the hour when we are / Trembling with tenderness" have more impact than the waste land imagery with which it begins and ends.

The undeveloped imagery of eyes in Part I is now, in the final version, rectified in Parts II and IV. Also, the play on the motif of kingdoms, whether capitalized or in lower case, in all four succeeding parts rounds out that aspect of the poem. Consequently, "We are the hollow men" is now simply the opening movement in a beautifully modulated dynamic structure. In the new context its only weakness is the pat repetition of the opening lines at the end. Part II, "Eyes I dare not meet in dreams," loses some of the direct poignancy of the opening poem of "Doris's Dream Songs": "Eyes that last I saw in tears"—assuming, that is, that Eliot considered including the latter poem at this point. I would hazard the suggestion that using it here would have committed him to a more confessional poem than he was ready to write. Because of the almost Tennysonian resonances of "Eyes that last I saw in tears," he would have faced the double problem of writing a frankly personal lyric sequence and breaking out of a tone that represents the perfection of a sensibility not quite his own.

But the pathway to critical hell is paved with such speculation. What we *have* is the splendid "Eyes I dare not meet in dreams." Though he has forgone the confessional dimension, Eliot gains an even more provocative imagery of missed sweetness at the start of this section and follows with metaphors of evasiveness in the face of any challenge to spiritual commitment that are grimmer in their horror than the chant of the stuffed figures of Part I. The squalor and misery of the representative speaker here come closest of any affect in the poem to its deepest pressure of feeling. The voice is that of essential anxiety:

> Let me be no nearer
> In death's dream kingdom
> Let me also wear
> Such deliberate disguises
> Rat's coat, crowskin, crossed staves
> In a field
> Behaving as the wind behaves
> No nearer—

> Not that final meeting
> In the twilight kingdom

There would have been some value in ending the sequence with Part III, "This is the dead land," in spite of the possible objections I have noted. But Eliot was determined—it is the driving purpose of virtually all his work after 1918 or so—to press the religious perspective. He does so in Part IV, "The eyes are not here." For a moment he echoes the *Inferno:* "In this last of meeting places / We grope together / And avoid speech / Gathered on this beach of the tumid river." And at the end he introduces a symbol of grace that is still somehow open to the hollow men, who are "Sightless, unless / The eyes reappear / As the perpetual star / Multifoliate rose." This forcing of the issue has been prefigured in the ending of Part I, but if the sequence had ended on this note its evangelical impulse would have been too nakedly exposed. Part V, *"Here we go round the prickly pear,"* rescues the work from this solemn reef by starting in a spirit of cynical buffoonery, with a nursery-rhyme parody. It then plunges into a chant, punctuated by a phrase from the Lord's Prayer and a tired commonplace, that is an elementary cry of personal frustration. The poem finally becomes reduced to a jumble of gibberish before the famous ending (another nursery-rhyme parody) proclaims the guttering out of a petty, pointless way of life. Pressing so hard in the fourth part has produced a counter-movement, of total humility. And now the self-contempt of the fifth part recalls the embarrassed distancing in many of the earlier poems. The devout, self-denigrating speaker, who cancels out any suspicion of hubris aroused by his vision of the "multifoliate rose" with the closing line *"Not with a bang but a whimper,"* has his hands full keeping the balance at the end. But he is succeeding.

I do not know of any other poet who gives one quite such an impression of a contest with himself, a struggle to humanize his attitudes and keep his art in tune with itself in just this way. The history of "Ash Wednesday" is similar to that of "The Hollow Men." Eliot published Part II first, under the title "Salutation," as a separate poem. It begins as the sprightliest of allegorical forays, combining the Dantean vision of the Lady as intercessor for the communicant with Ezekiel's vision in the Bible (*Ezekiel*, 37). Only a manically self-transcendent fantasist could fuse the courtly idealism of Dante's treatment of Beatrice with the wild energy of Ezekiel's words as Eliot does here. The speaker presents himself as a set of dry bones devoured by leopards and accepting their condition with bouncy joy, chirping their praise of the Lady and punning like vaudeville comedians and devoutly serious withal:

> And God said
> Shall these bones live? shall these
> Bones live? And that which had been contained
> In the bones (which were already dry) said chirping:
> Because of the goodness of this Lady
> And because of her loveliness, and because
> She honours the Virgin in meditation,
> We shine with brightness. And I who am here dissembled
> Proffer my deeds to oblivion, and my love
> To the posterity of the desert and the fruit of the gourd.
> It is this which recovers
> My guts the strings of my eyes and the indigestible portions
> Which the leopards reject. . . .

The long first stanza that includes these lines is followed by a prayer to the Lady in mystical terms—oxymora again, inducing a state of transcendence of the opposites named. The first few lines will be indicative:

> Lady of silences
> Calm and distressed
> Torn and most whole.

And after the prayer the bones take over again, while a subtle alteration of rhythm recalls the rapture of the song in Marvell's "Bermudas":

Under a juniper-tree the bones sang, scattered and shining
We are glad to be scattered, we did little good to each
    other . . .

What eventually came to be Part I was published a year later (in 1928) as *"Perch'io non spero."* It is a poem of personal renunciation and a prayer for mercy. The next year saw the appearance of Part III as *"Som de l'escalina,"* a nightmare poem in which powerful images of human grossness and decay are matched against images of romantic desire and sensuous sweetness beyond the protagonist's reach. The poem uses violent Dantean effects and projects the speaker's sufferings boldly. When Eliot assembled "Ash Wednesday" as a six-part sequence in 1930, he included this poem in the climactic pair at its center. Part IV ("Who walked between the violet and the violet") is the companion poem—at the far heights of Purgatory, close to heavenly tranquility, as opposed to the torment of Part III. It is one of Eliot's most winning efforts to suggest an atmosphere of quickened purity of response to everything gentle, redemptive, and loving, all embodied in a feminine figure like Mary whose memory persists in "this our exile":

The silent sister veiled in white and blue
Between the yews, behind the garden god,
Whose flute is breathless, bent her head and signed but spoke
    no word.

The two movements that follow are very largely a continuing prayer to this "veiled sister," so that Parts IV–VI form a more consistent group than Parts I–III. The dynamics of the first three parts results from the juxtaposing of three independently formed poems. Placed together, they set forth in a spirit of extreme self-renunciatory humility, then raise this tone to an ecstatic climax in the rhapsody of the bones (which harmonizes perfectly with the prayer for transcendence addressed to the Lady of Silences), and then become an intense closeup of the protagonist's sweating inner self in the purgatorial condition of his present moment. Part IV then swings us to the counter-vision I have described, which essentially controls the final two parts as well. Despite some incomparable brief lyric passages in these closing parts, they do not fully receive and contain or develop the earlier energies of the sequence. Rather, they present a problem similar to the one toward the end of "Little Gidding," for human kind cannot bear very much poetic litany, ordinarily, atop its other woes.

I would, however, call special attention to the first and the last of Eliot's "Ariel Poems": "Journey of the Magi" (1927) and "Marina" (1930). The "Ariel Poems" were a series of poetry pamphlets by various hands, published by Faber over a period of time. Eliot's contributions were made during the four years 1927–30, the same period as the development of "Ash Wednesday," and the two poems I have named are engaged with the same essential emotional sets as the longer work. They are less ambitious in scope but possibly more successful.

One reason may lie in the clearer, relatively more objectified, dramatic situation of the speakers, particularly in "Journey of the Magi." The speaker here is a king, one of the sages who came to Bethlehem with gifts for the infant Jesus. A number of years later we hear him telling about his journey, much in the manner of any querulous traveler. Mostly he describes difficulties—the discomfort, unfriendly people, commonplace scenes (glamorous

to us, however, because of their sacred and exotic associations). He and the other Magi were doubtful of the wisdom of what they were doing: they heard "voices singing in our ears, saying / That this was all folly." And the
actual visit to Jesus comes, in this account, as an an-
ticlimax:

>   and so we continued
>   And arrived at evening, not a moment too soon
>   Finding the place; it was (you may say) satisfactory.

The result, for this poor Magus and his fellows, was certainly not the bliss they may have expected; their experience has served merely to make their way of life intolerable:

>   We returned to our places, these Kingdoms,
>   But no longer at ease here, in the old dispensation,
>   With an alien people clutching their gods.
>   I should be glad of another death.

"Journey of the Magi" carries the same feeling as "Ash
Wednesday" of being caught up, not yet redeemed, in
the midst of ordinary life—and *"Life is very long,"* according to the closing part of "Ash Wednesday." At the
same time, the protagonists in both have had their tormenting glimpse of revelation or its possibility and can
never again be quite happy with their conditions. But
the shorter poem is a triumph of economy, moving un-
forcedly through its phases, blessedly free of the poet's
need to give equal time to his inner psyche and to the
compulsions of rhetoric and of devotion. A brilliant
stroke is the opening passage of quotation from a seven-
teenth-century sermon by Lancelot Andrewes. For reasons of rhythm, Eliot makes a couple of minute changes
in the language, but the significant change is from the

third person to the first. The passage from Andrewes has to do with the journey of the Magi and refers to them as "they." Eliot's speaker, naturally, says "we" instead. As a result, the poem begins with five lines of quotation that are stark in detail and win our sympathy at once. These lines, since they are in quotation-marks, have the effect of a document, an actual report by one of the Magi, and lend an air of authenticity to all the details of the journey that follow.

The long first stanza reinforces its beginning through an accumulation of grubby memories and regrets at forgoing "The summer palaces on slopes, the terraces, / And the silken girls bringing sherbet." In the briefer second stanza, this litany of travel memories continues. But now the details are isolated, unevaluated symbolic sights whose significance the speaker could not have known at the time—for instance, "six hands at an open door dicing for pieces of silver." Finally, the third stanza shows the speaker alone and embittered in his present moment, and longing for extinction and rebirth—though, in his agonized state, he calls it "another death." This agonized state, indeed, seems an incidental expense of Eliot's efforts to convert the feeling of spiritual emptiness in a waste of shame into the ambience of a dark night of the soul. A scoffer might conclude that seeing the light partially is the worst thing that can happen to a soul. The second "Ariel" poem, "A Song for Simeon," translates the sweetly grave story of Simeon in *Luke* 2:25–34 into something closer to sweet-*and*-sour. And the third "Ariel" poem, "Animula," moves from its touchingly autobiographical, rather sentimental account of the progress of the "simple soul" into melodramatic gloom capped (as often in Eliot's poems) by a final prayer for all who have perished disastrously and without vision. The initial charm of this poem, whose title and first line

(" 'Issues from the hand of God, the simple soul' ") recall
the Emperor Hadrian's "*Animula, vagula, blandula*" and a
specific passage in *Purgatorio*, XVI, on *"l'anima semplicet-
ta,"* lies in its evocation of innocence. The music of those
sources fills its sails at first. Then the sense of life itself, a
fairly privileged life as described here, becomes a painful
burden. Together with "the drug of dreams," it "curls
up the small soul" and grows heavier and heavier until
its weight sinks the poem.

It is a paradoxical fact—or so it seems in an age when
an enormous premium is put on the poetry of direct personal expression as opposed to poetry openly in communion with the whole poetic past—that an echo from some
traditional source often sends Eliot's poems soaring,
while introspective meditation drags them down toward redundancy and even verbosity. "Marina" draws a
great deal of its buoyancy and its elated longing from the
inspiration of Shakespeare's *Pericles*—specifically, the
scene (V,i) of Pericles's miraculous reunion with his
daughter Marina, whom he had thought dead. The poem
has affinities as well with "Ash Wednesday," Part IV
("Who walked between the violet and the violet"),
which also centers on a female figure embodying heart-
quickening purity—a vision of grace redeeming the protagonist from wasted years. Lovely and stirring as the
"Ash Wednesday" epiphany is, that in "Marina" is yet
more vivid. Shakespeare's energy has so infected Eliot's
style that the poem strikes with a bold intensity of image
and tone, liberated from the hesitancies of surface humility to which Eliot yielded so often. (Fortunately for
the poem, he did not base its mood on Lysimachus's
question about Pericles in the same scene: "Upon what
ground is his distemperature?") Although the vision appears and disappears before the speaker's eyes, it is elec-
tric with sensuous realization—

What is this face, less clear and clearer
The pulse in the arm, less strong and stronger—
Given or lent? more distant than stars and nearer than the eye

Whispers and small laughter between leaves and hurrying feet
Under sleep, where all the waters meet.

Bowsprit cracked with ice and paint cracked with heat.
I made this, I have forgotten
And remember.

Without going further into this very beautiful poem, I
would simply note that, like "Journey of the Magi," it
has probably benefited from being a sort of by-blow
of the struggle for an encompassing form in "Ash
Wednesday." Both poems offer objective correlatives for
the same complex emotional state that the sequence tries
to get in full perspective by juxtaposing its warring elements. I would be tempted to say that they are perfect
successes while the longer work is a brilliant failure, but
the other side of that particular coin is the necessary failure of sequences to achieve watertight structural perfection. The struggle for balance is the issue; and it is only
inadequate energy, or a waste of energy in redundancy,
or an absence of the instinct for dynamic progression
and modulation that can make a sequence fail formally.
All three of our poets give us abundant evidence of this
principle of balance, and all three have provided models
in plenty for their successors.

This point brings me to *Four Quartets*, a sequence that
begins almost perfectly with "Burnt Norton," continues
at a lower and often repetitive pitch in "East Coker"
and "The Dry Salvages," and flares up magnificently in
the first two movements of "Little Gidding" before guttering out. There is a mechanical parallelism in these
poems, each of which has five sections and a fairly clear

basic pattern with variations along the way. The fourth
section of each, for instance, presents a brief, concentrated passage, centered in a single image usually, that
expresses unresolved emotional crisis or in other ways
brings the emotion of the poem into focus. The first
movement of each is incantatory and usually has a visionary dimension or moment of epiphany such as we
saw in the speaker's illusion of "midwinter spring" in
"Little Gidding." In the final sections the speaker relates
his efforts as an artist working with language to the
problems of inducing and holding on to glimpses of eternity in the midst of time. The second and third sections
tend to be speculative and expansive. So there is a great
deal of external patterning, and the poems echo each
other motivationally and often in specific phrasing.

Nevertheless, one cannot really discern a continuously
orchestrated movement of feeling or awareness in an
aesthetic sense—only the surface design and the recurrent push to overcome depression and loss of morale.
The poems are not part of a single prolonged impulse or
predicament. "Burnt Norton" belongs with the period of
"Ash Wednesday" and just after. What I have called its
near-perfection has to do with its closeness in spirit to a
poem like "Marina" and its deepened tonalities after
Eliot's long-simmering, overdue reconsideration of his
search for an altered perspective, one less determined by
an almost cherished "nervous" condition. In the two
parts of *Sweeney Agonistes* (1932) he had let go and
created some wonderfully mordant comedy out of his
gift for parody and the morbid side of his personality,
comparable in its bizarrely satirical coloration to the
work of Bertolt Brecht in Germany. In the two poems put
together as *Coriolan* we can see him drawn into the orbit
of the political poetry of the 1930s, with his own twist,
naturally. But in "Burnt Norton," first published in *Col-*

lected Poems 1909–1935, there is a profound return, on new terms, to preoccupations of the 1927–30 period.

"East Coker" comes half a decade later, "The Dry Salvages" a year after that, and "Little Gidding" two years further on. On a smaller scale, and with some other significant differences, the problem is like that of trying to see the whole of *The Cantos* as a single poetic unit although Eliot's basic way of working was mosaic rather than monumental or in large sweeps. What we have, then, is essentially a key poem, "Burnt Norton," which serves as a model for a number of other poems following it and to which they refer in various ways—a series rather than a fully integral sequence.

"Burnt Norton" plunges directly into the old obsession and bedevilment: the tantalizing nudging of the spirit by illusion, memory, reverie, an atmosphere of loveliness—and the sudden apprehension of an immortal moment wherever one happens to be. At the very start the language seems appallingly abstract and philosophical, but then the rhythm takes hold: It rises to the rhythm of prayer, incantation, prophecy, especially in the ninth and tenth lines, and so turns the recital of abstractions into devout celebration of the immanence of eternity:

> Time present and time past
> Are both perhaps present in time future,
> And time future contained in time past.
> If all time is eternally present
> All time is unredeemable.
> What might have been is an abstraction
> Remaining a perpetual possibility
> Only in a world of speculation.
> What might have been and what has been
> Point to one end, which is always present.
> Footfalls echo in the memory
> Down the passage which we did not take

> Towards the door we never opened
> Into the rose-garden. My words echo
> Thus, in your mind.

As in "Marina," there is a perfection of technique here that grows out of unmediated immediacies of thought and feeling. The inert abstractions of metaphysical argument *can* provide one sort of affect, if a poet knows what he is doing. So considered, the first ten lines of this passage could play a poetic role even if there were no ritual dimension of the intonation of prayer. But that dimension gives vitality to the lines and makes their subtle notes of qualification ("perhaps," the ambiguous placement of "only") contributory to the humble timbre of the prayer. The communicant is praising the all-encompassment of God, the eternal principle, and at the same time denying himself the right to speak too positively. And he is leaving the question open whether or not "What might have been" retains its potentiality even after the event—hence that ambiguous use of "only." I should add that anyone writing a passage like this is aware of the charming trick of language he is playing and is therefore exercising considerable wit. So the passage, contrary to every appearance, has its own ebullience and gaiety as well.

Nor does the stanza end with the tenth line. Once the hypnotic chant has done its work, it is reembodied in the memory of a visit to a rose-garden, something that might have happened but never did and yet sticks in the mind. The speaker knows we all have such "memories" and raises the question why it should be so:

> But to what purpose
> Disturbing the dust on a bowl of rose-leaves
> I do not know.

He does know, actually. The answer was given in lines 1–10. In raising the question, too, he has introduced a new image into the poem—"disturbing the dust on a bowl of rose-leaves." It is an image of the passage of time and of the mind's accumulation of past events and hopes, and also of the "disturbance" of evocative memory. And then the rest of Part I moves into an extended moment of pure vision. We are taken into a rose-garden paradise, that imagined reality in which all delight arises out of its absence, in a plethora of oxymora: "unheard music hidden in the shrubbery," "the unseen eyebeam," a dry pool "filled with water out of sunlight" where "the lotos rose, quietly, quietly." Perhaps all this has arisen from the sight of a dust-covered bowl of rose-leaves—or so the speaker may be hinting. But we have been to a place where childish disappointment is undone (as in Pericles's memory of his daughter playing, in "Marina"):

> the leaves were full of children,
> Hidden excitedly, containing laughter.

It is a vision that cannot be sustained. As the small annunciatory bird that has urged us into the garden and then hurries us out insists, "Human kind / Cannot bear very much reality." But the copresence of the eternal has been confirmed, and Part I ends with a partial reprise of the opening incantation.

Very few things in life or poetry are as satisfying as this opening movement of "Burnt Norton." Certainly Part II is not. It begins as though it might be, with a fifteen-line celebration of the Great Chain of Being whereby all things small and large are figured in one another—

> The dance along the artery
> The circulation of the lymph
> Are figured in the drift of stars

In this cosmic design all abstract patterns are concrete and alive—a further warrant that what the mind conceives is a reflex of total reality. There is joy at transcendence in this passage, but of a special kind—anything but sentimental. Not human needs and feelings but impersonal process and principle are being exalted:

> The trilling wire in the blood
> Sings below inveterate scars
> Appeasing long forgotten wars.

A thrill of cold excitement prevails here. Part I has converted humanized abstraction into a vision of sweet triumph over mortality and loss, but the vision of process in Part II has the distant, not necessarily reassuring beauty of stars in the clear night sky. (The star-imagery I use here simply echoes Eliot's.) The same essential contrast, Yeatsian in its reciprocities, of human and nonhuman transcendence returns in exquisitely compressed form in Part IV. Meanwhile, however, most of the rest of Part II experiments prosily with a loose, expository verse that wreaks havoc with the tension and tonal authority of the poem for a while (as it does in the other poems of the sequence as well). It is interesting that Eliot feels free to try such lines as these:

> Neither movement from nor towards,
> Neither ascent nor decline. Except for the point, the still point,
> There would be no dance, and there is only the dance.
> I can only say, *there* we have been: but I cannot say where.
> And I cannot say, how long, for that is to place it in time.

One finds this verse-line interesting for the wrong reason—not in itself but because only complacency would permit a writer of such talents to let his poem go slack this way just to hammer home a doctrinal point already made. (Of course, he meant to get a tone at once confidential, relaxed, and seriously thoughtful, but it is the same slack line that makes much of his drama poetically boring.) Fortunately, the effect is less destructive in "Burnt Norton" than in succeeding quartets. Part II ends by somewhat retrieving the atmosphere of the poem's beginning:

> To be conscious is not to be in time
> But only in time can the moment in the rose-garden,
> The moment in the arbour where the rain beat,
> The moment in the draughty church at smokefall
> Be remembered; involved with past and future.
> Only through time time is conquered.

It does not quite work. The prose-dreariness is still present in this second time-chant despite the invocation of other moments of epiphany, real or desired. We have been prepared for Part III, the depressive portion of the poem, in the wrong way. Yet the poem's strengths are such that it magnificently survives the letdown in Part II.

Part III plunges us at once into a negative epiphany in the tunnels of the London underground railway—as powerful an evocation of everlasting hell as the rose-garden scene in Part I is of paradise. Slowly the passage recalls moments in the *Inferno,* not so much through deliberate verbal echoing as through the images of whirling wind and of "unhealthy souls" riding in the trains and—especially—through the increasing gloom of the phrasing. Part IV then seems to arise from the depths of this gloom in a pure impulse of questioning music that contains its own reply. Its pivotal images restore a balance in what is surely the most beautiful of the concentrated, imagistic centers in the sequence. It begins with a

near-doggerel couplet, a compressed dirge expressing
the speaker's dark night of the soul. Then follows a
series of strange questions, full of pathos and hubris at
one and the same time. The speaker's hopeless desire for
an undeniably heavenly sign—the miraculous turning to
"us" of sunflower, clematis, and yew in a revelatory
transference of heliotropic magnetism to mortal men (the
true sun having disappeared)—enters the poem in the
form of these questions. The self-ironic hubris of this
thought is bitterly depressive, as we see in the final
image in the series of questions: "Chill / Fingers of yew
be curled / Down on us?" But the reply that follows, the
magnificent cluster of images in the final sentence,
counters the despair by implying that revelation need
not come through a personal response to the individual
suppliant. Instead, divinity reveals itself impersonally—
as in the vision of transcendence beginning Part II, but
here more promising because of the imagery of light and
annunciation and "answering." All this is developed in
ten lines of shifting affects that take the mood from the
depths to a kind of transport:

> Time and the bell have buried the day,
> The black cloud carries the sun away.
> Will the sunflower turn to us, will the clematis
> Stray down, bend to us; tendril and spray
> Clutch and cling?
> Chill
> Fingers of yew be curled
> Down on us? After the kingfisher's wing
> Has answered light to light, and is silent, the light is still
> At the still point of the turning world.

The beginning of Part V reverts to despair: the poet's
loving despair over his art. Hubristic again, he desires a
perfection beyond his perishable medium. The ecstasy of

the illusion of success is contradicted, however, by the way words "decay with imprecision." The poem ends in a balancing of tones and motifs previously introduced. An endlessly suggestive structure, it is (with the first two parts of "Little Gidding") the high point of Eliot's writing after "The Waste Land." In it, he has altered the terms of his work and broadened his affective range, virtually completing his explorations in form.

Chapter 8

Continuities:
LESSONS OF THE MASTERS

Yeats, Pound, and Eliot stand out among the shapers of modern poetry in English. Unquestionably there are other figures who could readily be ranged alongside them—the names are well known, and I trust that my critical emphasis here will not be taken as an implied depreciation. Among them are James Joyce, the great prose poet of the age although not usually thought of in quite that way. And there is William Carlos Williams, who helped so in turning the soil for a new cultivation of American poetic idiom. Because of his reciprocities with Pound and Eliot, I shall certainly have a few things to say about him in this final chapter.

First, though, I wish simply to suggest some general ways in which our three poets are a continuing presence. I have already offered the main evidence, the poems themselves when we engage ourselves with them—or better, lose ourselves in them—in detail. All poetry of any quality becomes modern once we do so. Initial barriers of idom and attitude suddenly cease to exist (though we may flatter ourselves on this score too soon, I admit). This is what happens to working poets all the time when they put themselves in touch with poetry of past ages in an assimilative process that intimately recovers states of human awareness. The critic is well advised not to pass judgment on this process of communion but to try his feeble sympathetic best to be instructed in what the poets are doing by what they write.

I shall return to his matter of using the past. Our overview here has to do with shifts of sensibility and poetic method embodied in the work of Yeats, Pound, and Eliot. Their main artistic contribution is the modulation toward a poetry of open process, largely presentative, which tends toward a balancing of volatile emotional states. All are inconsistent in this respect; and, except in his experiments with sequences, Yeats is the least "advanced"—at any rate on the surface. We are talking about a significant evolutionary change of which the practitioners are only incompletely conscious (and the theorists almost completely unconscious, so that the main developments occur by a sort of instinctive collusion among the most highly sensitized poets at any given moment). An important part of the balancing in their work is enforced by their deep sense of traditional form and its values. It is clear, after all, that modern poetry as a whole, up to this very moment, has room for work as completely open and undisciplined as Robert Creeley's *A Day Book* side by side with Robert Lowell's attempt to control the chaos of his associative stream by writing his *Notebook* in a series of "unrhymed blank verse sonnets." Their meter, says Lowell, "is fairly strict at first and elsewhere, but often corrupts . . . to the freedom of prose."* These titles hardly represent the ex-

---

* Robert Lowell, *Notebook* (New York: Farrar, Straus and Giroux, 1970), p. 263.

treme limits on either side, if one takes into account the fairly tight, rather conventional forms often employed by a large number of respected poets—Richard Wilbur, Philip Larkin, and Stanley Kunitz, for instance—on the one hand and the proliferations of Imamu Amiri Baraka, Jeff Nuttall, and Peter Redgrove (in his prose-poetry) on the other.

Poetry of open process is closely linked to the special stress on high points of intensity that characterizes the work of our three poets and for a while dominated Pound's poetic almost exclusively. The Imagist movement, from this standpoint, was simply a way of dramatizing this stress by calling attention to its most obvious vehicle, the single image as a center of emotive concentration—"an intellectual and emotional complex in an instant of time," as Pound put it so memorably. Any tonal effect serves the same purpose by the kind of vibration it starts. Giving special attention to the image was basically a way of calling attention to the need for hard centers of reference evocative of passionate and heightened realization. "Tone poems" would not be enough. I have quoted Yeats on the subject: "I had begun to get rid of everything that is not, whether in lyric or dramatic poetry, in some sense character in action; a pause in the midst of action perhaps, but action always its end and theme." Eliot's famous definition of the "objective correlative" has the same purpose, to point a way to an actively presentative poetry based on concrete emotional states—"a set of objects, a situation, a chain of events which shall be the formula of that *particular* emotion; such that, when the external facts, which must terminate in sensory experience, are given, the emotion is immediately evoked." Our poets were insisting on the ultimate human significance of the kind of poetry they were after. They wished to put pure aestheticism, toward which the poetry of Yeats's youth (for Pound and Eliot the poetry of a parent generation) was tending, to a more rigorous service—a paradoxical endeavor that led to the great flowering of lyric poetry after World War I.

That volatile state I have mentioned as characteristic of the heights of their work is a state of ultimate human readiness, vulnerability, openness. The effort toward it goes naturally with the evolution of the modern poetic sequence and the constant struggle for encompassing form that the making of a sequence entails. Self-indulgence shows up very quickly in the context of such an aim. We have seen both Pound and Eliot marking time in tendentious and rhetorical passages without sufficient emotive quickening. A good deal of the later Wallace Stevens suffers from overexpanded musing with virtually no intensity, and a fair amount of John Ashbery's writing is an endless proliferation of tones without focus. Openness is hardly an end in itself, even when the sensibility at work is as entranced with itself as in these two poets. Nevertheless, the experiments of Yeats, Pound, and Eliot probably made this problem inevitable with highly gifted poets who have infinite patience and can burn quietly along forever in their low-flickering way. But it was a poetry of passionate intensity, close to the life out of which it springs and inspired to match the greatness of the past, that those experiments set out to create.

Here I wish to return to the matter of the use of the past, looking once again to the Odyssean model as conceived and used by Pound. This model is a key to a great deal. It takes us into all the implications of significantly open process—the risks of sailing into the unknown, using images and other radiant centers as points of reference ("periplum") rather than relying on conventional narrative or logical structure. And it uses the past as a living pressure and presence, a source of strength rather than anxiety. The normal poetic position—from a poet's point of view—is that communion with the sensibilities of the past is necessary both to self-location and to learning what it is to explore the hitherto unknown.

The communion, obviously, is not a matter of reference to works of the past or simple echoing of phrases, motifs, or thoughts. Like Joyce's in *Ulysses,* Pound's sensibility and starting-point remain his own. Where translation is involved, his effort to remain in touch with the essential tone and sound of his original while he is creating a genuine, new poem in his own language is the most direct communion possible. It is an accommodation between two sets of sensibility, the recovery of the living voice of another culture in another age: an "adaptation" and a "homage," to use two of Pound's terms.

But the use of the past has many subtler aspects, and is inseparable from experimentation that counts. What, in fact, does it mean for poetry to "advance"? to "experiment"? I do not think that in poetry, any more than in science, the repetition of a method that someone else has already employed successfully can be considered an experiment in any sense but that of a classroom exercise or of a practitioner's confirmation of techniques. If we use the good old touchstone method, and if we know what the touchstones are, it should not be hard to sort out the question of the originality of a given piece or mode of work. Of course, the question is complicated by qualitative considerations of the precision and sensitivity of phrasing and general form.

Take, for instance, a classic—I should say, *"secret* classic"—of the modern age like Pound's Canto 39, written over forty years ago. It is one culmination of a method Pound had been developing for fifteen years or more. I cannot imagine that a poet who has at all allowed himself to be instructed by *The Cantos* could fail to pick up important clues from Canto 39. Looking at it first in the simplest way, it is a constellation of rather brilliant lyric and imagistic passages, somehow linked by allusions to events in the *Odyssey*, to certain Latin and medieval lyric motifs, to sexual cosmogenies in mythic tradition, and to kinds of private experience barely hinted at. Its frank sensuality comes through as purely as anything in the language. Pound learned from Latin and Provençal poetry and from such a poet as Villon to use the elementary language of sex unselfconsciously and rightly in context, so that it gets past—beyond—the compulsiveness and sensationalism of mere pornography. Suddenly he lifts the faintly pornographic veil of insidious suggestiveness that flutters like a figleaf over so much of the best nineteenth-century poetry, with its repressions and reticences and strange hints of darkness and evil. Here is how the opening section of the poem goes:

> Desolate is the roof where the cat sat,
> Desolate is the iron rail that he walked
> And the corner post whence he greeted the sunrise.
> In hill path: "thkk, thgk"
>   of the loom
> "Thgk, thkk" and the sharp sound of a song
>   under olives
> When I lay in the ingle of Circe
> I heard a song of that kind.
>   Fat panther lay by me
> Girls talked there of fucking, beasts talked there of eating,
> All heavy with sleep, fucked girls and fat leopards,
> Lions loggy with Circe's tisane,
> Girls leery with Circe's tisane
>   κακὰ φάρμακ' ἔδοκεν
>   kaka pharmak edōken

Here, then, is a poem saturated with realizations of the sexual principle as experience, both literally physical and as the informing element of poetry, song, and myth.

The marvelous opening passage begins with the imagistic closeup of the scene where the cat lived his happy night. Except for the absolute clarity of its language and of its pictured scene, that three-line closeup might be a full-length early poem by Robert Creeley—especially if we accept its tone of wry desolation as expressing the speaker's own postcoital sadness. The speaker then changes masks and becomes Odysseus, or one who thinks of himself as Odysseus in the particular context of his situation. He has been with a woman—in that sense has been Odysseus with Circe—and he brings the very essence of happy satiety, a stupefied utter enchantment of replete sensuality, into the foreground, framing it by the Homeric phrase that is repeated like a refrain (*kaka pharmak edōken*—she had given them dreadful drugs).

At this late point, I shall not follow the poem through any further, or do more than mention its indicativeness of the whole method of *The Cantos:* the projection of lines and fields of association in relation to certain radiating centers of value and of affect. Essentially, most experimental method that interests us today—even the self-interferences in poets like Robert Duncan and Charles Olson that are intended to strangle rhetoric and to untrack poetic structuring—is fully anticipated in *The Cantos.* What is it that is being experimented with? First of all, Romantic absorption in the reciprocities of subjective and objective. Secondly, the possibilities implicit in the open sequences of Whitman and other forerunners. Thirdly, the adaptation of lyric technique and Symbolist preoccupations to longer structures with epic pretensions. Incidental to these, a number of formal and thematic adjustments and changes in poetic diction: rhythmic improvisations; assimilation of more and more supposedly unpoetic words and modes of expression; visual arrangements that are aspects of internal structure rather than superficial elegances; the use of casual or purely functional cultural objects and technological devices (comic strips, mechanical cranes, or whatever) not as symbols of the age but as objects of direct contemplation, as though they were Grecian urns or Wordsworthian hills. Exploring some of these lines of possibility has become for many poets what "research" means for a certain kind of scholar: accumulation of more and more data toward the finally redundant ends of mere process. I do not pretend that we are dealing with the predictable, however. We all know that individual voice and wit and imagination can change what would ordinarily be stale and unprofitable into something that really tells. Poets who keep testing the limits of the art by using language virtually devoid of nervous tension and by interrupting a lyric tone, when it does begin to emerge, with bits of data, found poetry, and prose forays that are deliberately undistinguished and even stumbling run the risk of ending with very little that is poetically memorable. Gary Snyder's work, sensitive as it can be, is an example. Yet these seem transitional problems.

In their separate ways, but also by watching each other's trials, our three poets taught themselves to see the structure of a sequence as that of a lyric poem writ large. The position could not have evolved without the poets' having become accustomed to think in terms of centers of intensity when writing on a smaller scale. In our own moment, even fairly conventional poetry tries to follow Keats's advice—"load every rift with ore"—and to reflect an alert and confessionally forthcoming personality. The lessons of structure, though, have not been so well learned. I have already mentioned the tendency to write sequences as strings of poems arranged simply in order of composition, or even in journal or diary form.

Olson's *The Maximus Poems,* Creeley's *A Day Book,* Lowell's *Notebook,* and Adrienne Rich's *The Blue Ghazals*
are basically so ordered, except for small thematic groupings. Despite considerable stylistic differences, they
have in common their reference to the speaking personality in the poem as its unifying center. That speaking
personality is the poet's empirical self, objectified as a
mirror-image in the sequences but lyrically unassimi-
lated. The sequences rely on the poet's personality as sufficiently interesting, sufficiently remarkable in its suffering and perceptiveness and powers of thought and
observation, to justify a long work that bloweth wherever its wandering footstep or attention listeth. The assumption is that sheer drifting along, and the variations
of theme and feeling time provides, will create structure
enough. This is a dubious assumption. Lowell several
times reordered, divided, and shuffled his *Notebook,* in
varying editions with different titles, in search of something more satisfactory. All these works (unlike Lowell's earlier *Life Studies*) are far more impressive at isolated points along the way than as organic wholes.

The influence of Eliot—of the way he worked in "The
Waste Land" but also the way he evolved his earlier
sequences—seems to me strongly at work in all these
poets. It is most surprising, I think, in Olson, Creeley,
and other Black Mountain poets, for they so firmly rejected him in theory. They felt closer to Pound and closest to Williams, who had violently repudiated Eliot's influence as inimical to the main task: making a poetry out
of American speech and its rhythms. The new poetry,
Williams held, must satisfy the American need for a
"common language" so that a shared candor between
people could emerge in the context of a shared history
and a shared relation to American cultural realities. But
Williams—especially in *Paterson,* his great sequence

which confronts these problems—had far more in common with the poetics of Eliot, and with those of Pound and Yeats as well, than he or many of his followers would ordinarily recognize. Thus, while his emphasis is certainly local and American, the persona he presents in the opening book of *Paterson* is an older version of Lusty Juventus in Canto 29, and is even shown in a similar romantic scene. But he is a dweller in the waste land as well.

Published just about a quarter-century after "The Waste Land" (in 1946), Book I of *Paterson* is in the voice of an alienated, suffering man, complete with sexual malaise, and readily comparable with the sensibility of Eliot's sequence. Both works are obsessed by our lost connections with the meaningful past and by the squalor of ordinary lives alike indifferent to exalted human vision and to the beauty of the landscape and the history buried in it. Both of them, too, reflect the same mixture of ruthless directness and aesthetic fastidiousness.

An interesting if elusive connection is that Eliot's improvisatory method, which arose in his practice simply from his casting about among possible ways of combining affects to achieve a significant structure, is objectified as a conscious principle of composition by Williams. If we look at the poetic "Preface" to *Paterson,* the opening section is most suggestive:

"Rigor of beauty is the quest. But how will you find beauty when it is locked in the mind past all remonstrance?"

> To make a start,
> out of particulars
> and make them general, rolling
> up the sum, by defective means—
> Sniffing the trees,
> just another dog

among a lot of dogs. What
else is there? And to do?
The rest have run out—
after the rabbits.
Only the lame stands—on
three legs. Scratch front and back.
Deceive and eat. Dig
a musty bone.

For the beginning is assuredly
the end—since we know nothing, pure
and simple, beyond
our own complexities.

Yet there is
no return: rolling up out of chaos,
a nine months' wonder, the city
the man, an identity—it can't be
otherwise—an
interpenetration, both ways. . . .

The epigraph to this passage is distinctly Williams's
own, both in style and thought. Yet it is also a remote
echo of Pound's French epigraph, attributed to one
"Caid Ali," at the head of Poem II in "Mauberley
(1920)"—which, in turn, is a play on the use of obscure
epigraphs by Eliot and others. Putting his thought this
way, as a quotation, was a whimsy of Pound's. But the
thought itself, connecting one's ability to understand
love to one's aesthetic sensibilities, was dead serious:
*"S'ils ne comprennent pas la poésie, s'ils ne sentent pas la
musique, qu'est ce qu'ils peuvent comprendre de cette passion . . .?"* This question is an essential, underlying
concern of *Paterson*.

In the first stanza of the "Preface," we see Williams
spelling out the improvisatory method he will employ.
He projects it in an image-complex literally based on the

idea that, to write this sequence, he must start from scratch. The knowledge that this is painful labor, the feeling of being inferior to the other "dogs" (that he is "lame" and starting out long after the others have "run out"), and the self-depreciation and buffoonery of the stanza, are connections with Eliot despite the radically different kind of phrasing William employs. Curiously, in the next stanza, his phrasing at the start ("For the beginning is assuredly / the end") echoes a repeated motif in *Four Quartets,* especially the sentence beginning both stanzas in the opening movement of "East Coker": "In my beginning is my end." Even the perplexed realization that "we know nothing . . . beyond our own complexities" may be a reflex of the "lost Coriolanus" passage about the imprisonment we suffer within ourselves near the end of "The Waste Land."

Eliot's writing was so deeply absorbed by his fellow-poets, perhaps especially by those who wished to resist his influence and yet to work on as serious or monumental a level, that they could not help being infected with his insidious tones of cultural malaise, self-undercutting, and private misery. This was a triumph of his extraordinary ear. A contemporary as responsive to language and rhythms as Williams was bound to be possessed by Eliot's writing to some degree at least. This was even truer of younger poets who had studied Eliot and Eliot-criticism and very possibly had paid special attention to him as secondary-school and university students.

Of course, I have been talking about the later Williams. The first book of *Paterson* appeared when he was sixty-three (strange coincidence of the age at which he, like Yeats and Pound, came to the work of his richest maturity), and the Black Mountain poets began to be felt five years or more later. There was a long germinative period of modern poetry before World War II, however.

Between the early impact of Pound and Eliot, coinciding
with the maturing of Yeats during and after World War I,
and the works I have just been discussing, several generations of modern poets flourished. The extremely vital
interim writing of Hart Crane, the Stevens of *Harmonium*
and the next few volumes, the Auden generation in England and America, and others, most of them powerfully
nourished on the writing of Yeats, Pound, and Eliot,
created the matrix out of which our poetry has hardly yet
emerged. I would call attention to such works as Basil
Bunting's *Briggflatts,* Ted Hughes's *Crow,* Galway Kinnell's *The Book of Nightmares,* and Ramon Guthrie's *Maximum Security Ward,* all fairly recent, as persuasive evidence of the fact.

Earlier on, I mentioned the fact that even the most
conventional modern lyric poetry of any quality bears
witness to the centrality of intensity, rather than sen-
timent or moralizing, as its chief value. We should, naturally, recognize that this is an international phenomenon
except in official art. Yeats, Pound, and Eliot do not account for the poetry of Lorca or Michel or Voznesensky,
important transmitters of international currents though
the two Americans were. Any English-speaking poet
who wishes may open himself to the poetry of other lan-
guages, and many have done so. And yet the magnetism
of sensibilities that show the way is such that the chan-
nels they open remain the major ones. The most influen-
tial models in current British verse, for instance, are—
despite a huge American impact after about 1965—W. H.
Auden, William Empson, and Philip Larkin. Behind
them, inevitably, the real force is Yeats—not Yeats the
mystical symbolist and passionate explorer of elemental
reality but Yeats the advocate of straightforward syntax
and of the use of intelligence as an active poetic energy.
The stripped-down Yeats who shows in the marriage-
poems has more power than these writers usually show,

but they too are essentially *presenting* a critical human awareness, often with a great deal of wit that keeps an equal amount of emotion under control. Larkin's "Talking in Bed" is a perfect instance both of these characteristics and of the difference between Yeats's Romantic dismay at the failure of sexual communication and the contemporary English poet's wrily helpless response:

> Talking in bed ought to be easiest,
> Lying together there goes back so far,
> An emblem of two people being honest.
>
> Yet more and more time passes silently.
> Outside, the wind's complete unrest
> Builds and disperses clouds about the sky,
>
> And dark towns heap up on the horizon.
> None of this cares for us. Nothing shows why
> At this unique distance from isolation
>
> It becomes still more difficult to find
> Words at once true and kind,
> Or not untrue and not unkind.

Poetry of power, such as we find in Ted Hughes's "Pike" or in a number of the sections in his overloaded but important sequence *Crow,* is rare in modern England and tends to be Yeatsian in its formal control. In Hughes's writing the tremendous, unfocused nervous drive is rarely given direct personal expression, even in the oblique manner of Larkin's "Talking in Bed." Rather, it is both projected and displaced by the images of animal ferocity and the surrealistic dream-scenarios that fill his pages. Confessional poetry that fuses the nervous energy of Eliot's struggle for inner order with Yeats's methods is more likely to be found in such contemporary Irish work as Austin Clarke's *Mnemosyne Lay in Dust* and the sequences of Thomas Kinsella and John Montague.

But I have not meant to survey all of current poetry—

only to suggest its continuities with the work of our three masters. The ripples of connection are innumerable. If I were to devote myself to the sexual and political dimensions alone, whether the subtler permutations or the more obvious aspects of the modern urge toward ever greater frankness and openness to the forbidden and the revolutionary, I should require another volume of at least equal length. Our poetry is necessarily responsive to the vast underground volcanic forces changing our lives so deeply in this century—our sense of the world and our individual expectations, and indeed the basis of our most intimate personal lives. The particular ideological biases of our three poets are far less significant than their sense of this volatile condition and their recognition of the kinds of extension and modification of their art necessary to meet the new demands. Genius such as theirs is sufficient unto itself, yet spills over into the art following after it and is illuminated by that art in countless unforeseen ways.

Note

My primary texts of reference are the following:

T. S. Eliot, *Collected Poems 1909-1962* (New York: Harcourt, Brace & World; London: Faber and Faber, 1963).

———, *The Waste Land: A Facsimile and Transcript of the Original Drafts Including the Annotations of Ezra Pound,* edited and with an introduction by Valerie Eliot (New York: Harcourt Brace Jovanovich, 1971).

Ezra Pound, *The Cantos* (New York: New Directions, 1970; London: Faber and Faber, 1975). (These editions of Cantos 1-117 are not identical.)

———, *Personae: The Collected Shorter Poems* (New York: New Directions, 1949).

William Butler Yeats, *The Collected Poems* (London: Macmillan, 1950; New York: Macmillan ["Definitive Edition"], 1956).

———, *The Variorum Edition of the Poems* (New York: Macmillan, 1957).

In Chapter 8 ("Continuities: Lessons of the Masters," pp. 204 ff), reference is made to the following specific works:

Basil Bunting, *Briggflatts: An Autobiography* (London: Fulcrum Press, 1966).

Austin Clarke, *Mnemosyne Lay in Dust* [in *Collected Poems* (Dublin: Dolmen Press; New York and London: Oxford University Press, 1974)].

Robert Creeley, *A Day Book* (New York: Charles Scribner's Sons, 1972).

Ramon Guthrie, *Maximum Security Ward* (New York: Farrar, Straus & Giroux, 1970).

Ted Hughes, *Crow* (New York: Harper & Row, 1971).

Galway Kinnell, *The Book of Nightmares* (Boston: Houghton Mifflin, 1971).

Philip Larkin, "Talking in Bed" [in *The Whitsun Weddings* (London: Faber and Faber, 1964)].

Robert Lowell, *Notebook* (New York: Farrar, Straus & Giroux, 1970). The first version of this book was *Notebook 1967-68* (1969), and in 1973 three related volumes appeared: *The Dolphin, History,* and *For Lizzie and Harriet,* all from the same publisher. (See comment on p. 212.)

Charles Olson, *The Maximus Poems* (New York: Jargon/Corinth, 1960).

———, *The Maximus Poems IV, V, VI* (New York: Grossman; London: Goliard, 1968).

Adrienne Rich, *The Blue Ghazals* [in *The Will to Change* (New York: W. W. Norton, 1971)].

William Carlos Williams, *Paterson* (New York: New Directions, 1963).

Index